PAREIDOLIA

NOUN

PAR·EI·DO·LIA ˌPER-ˌĪ-ˈDŌ-LĒ-Ə -ˈDŌL-YƏ

THE TENDENCY TO PERCEIVE A SPECIFIC, OFTEN MEANINGFUL

IMAGE IN A RANDOM OR AMBIGUOUS VISUAL PATTERN

THE PHOTOS ON THE LEFT ARE UNRETOUCHED

THE PHOTOS ON THE RIGHT HAVE BEEN PRINTED AND SCRIBBLED ON WITH
A MARKER, SO YOU CAN SEE THE FACES TOO

DO YOU SEE THEM?

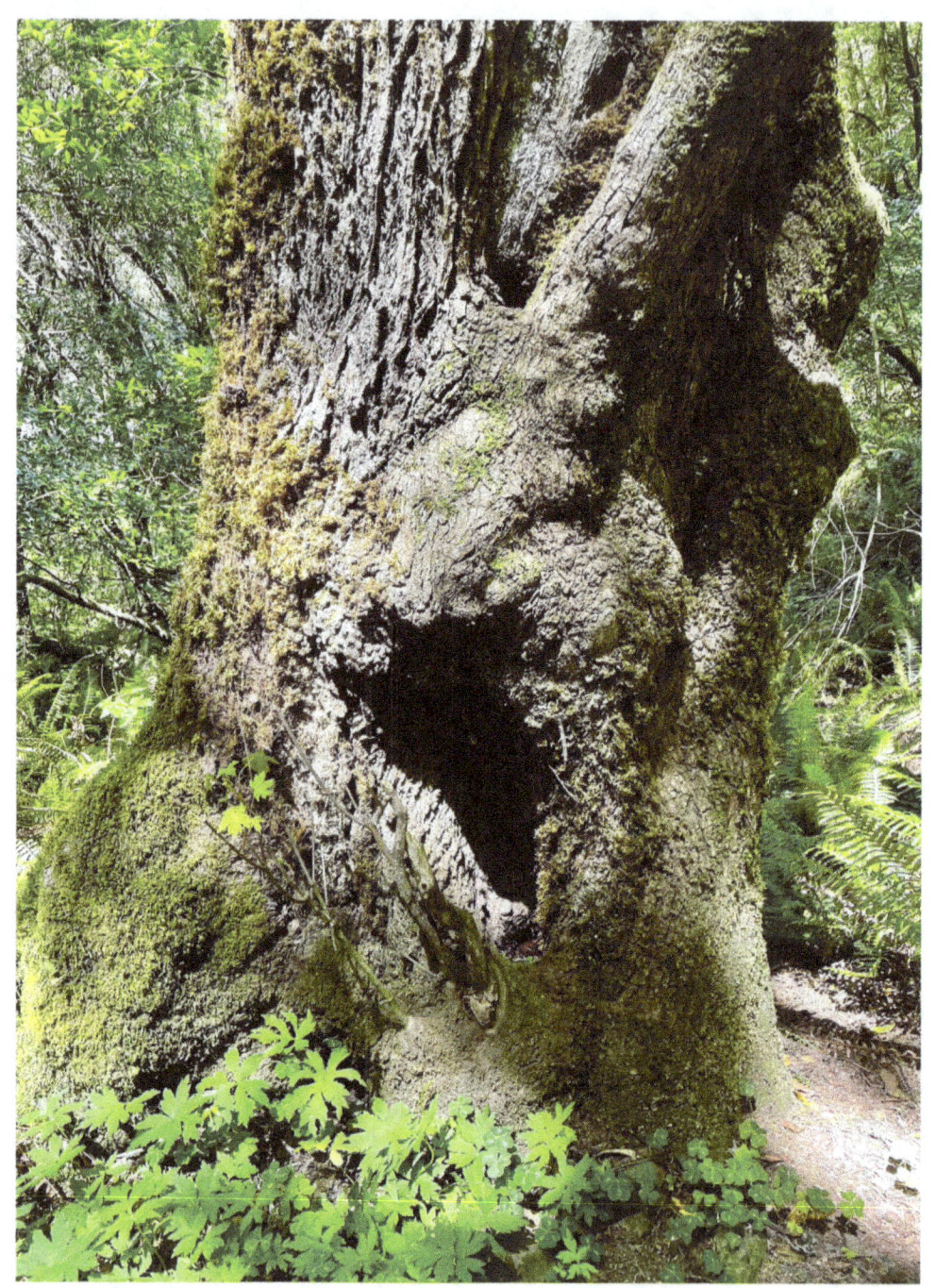

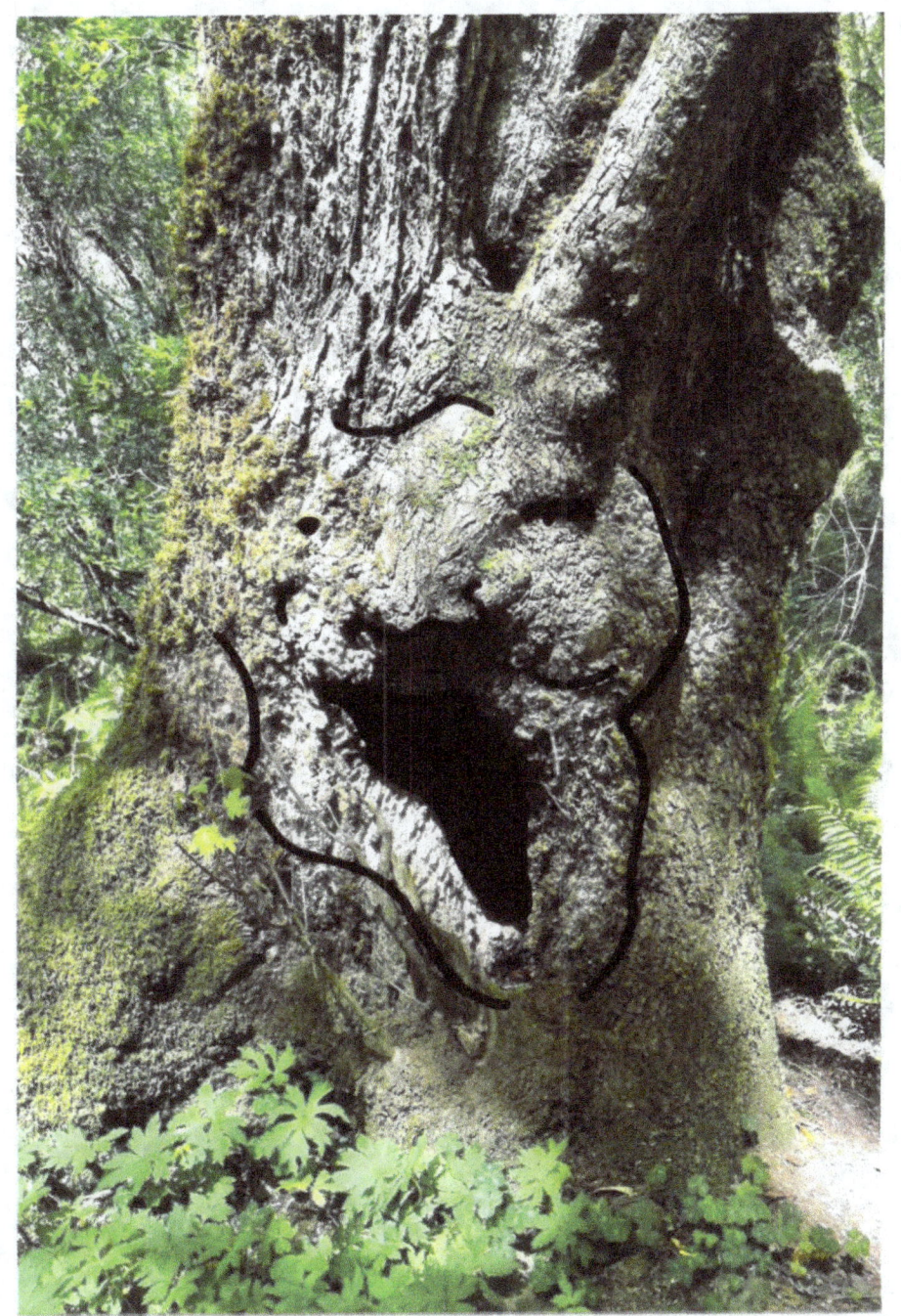

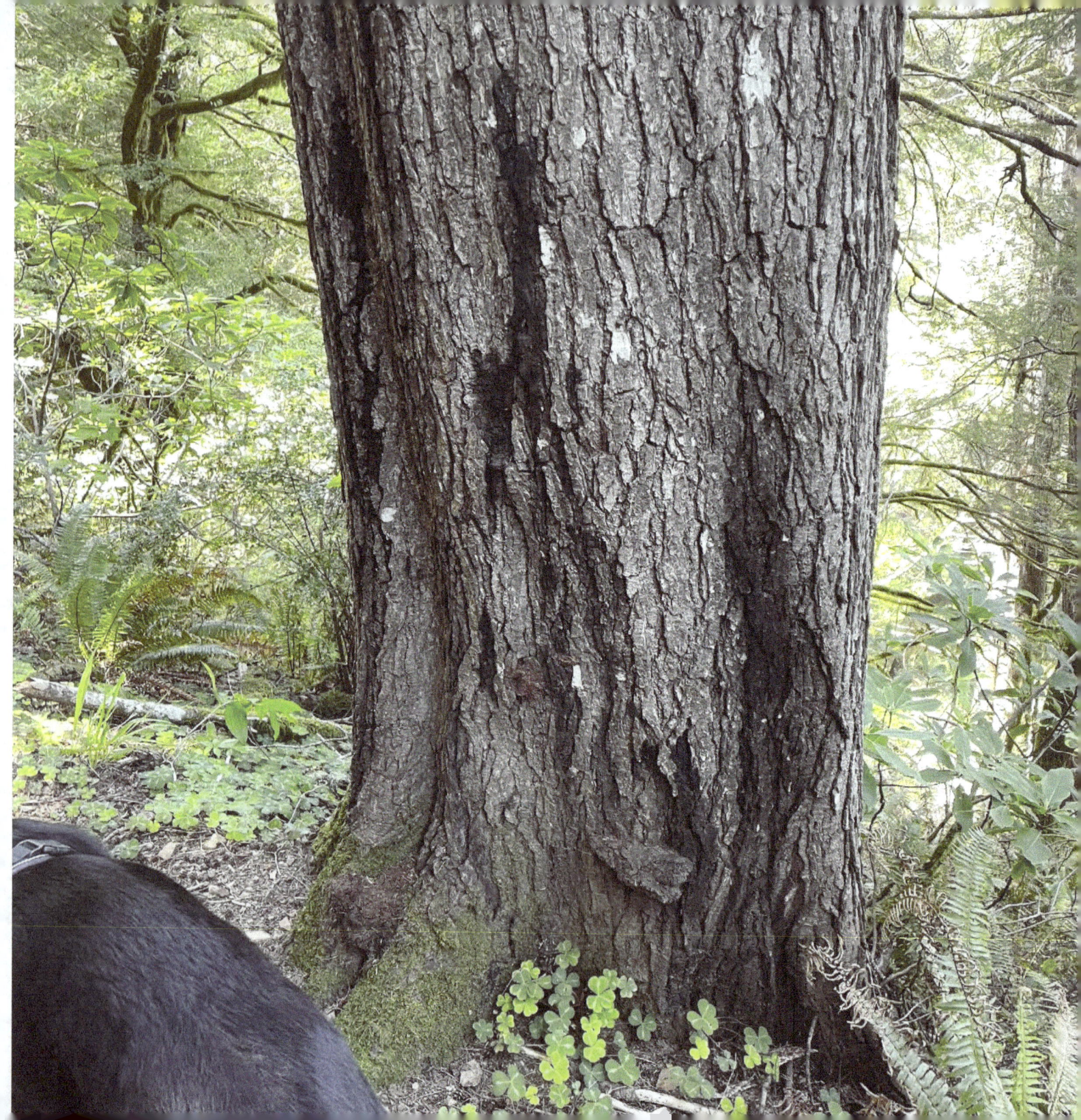

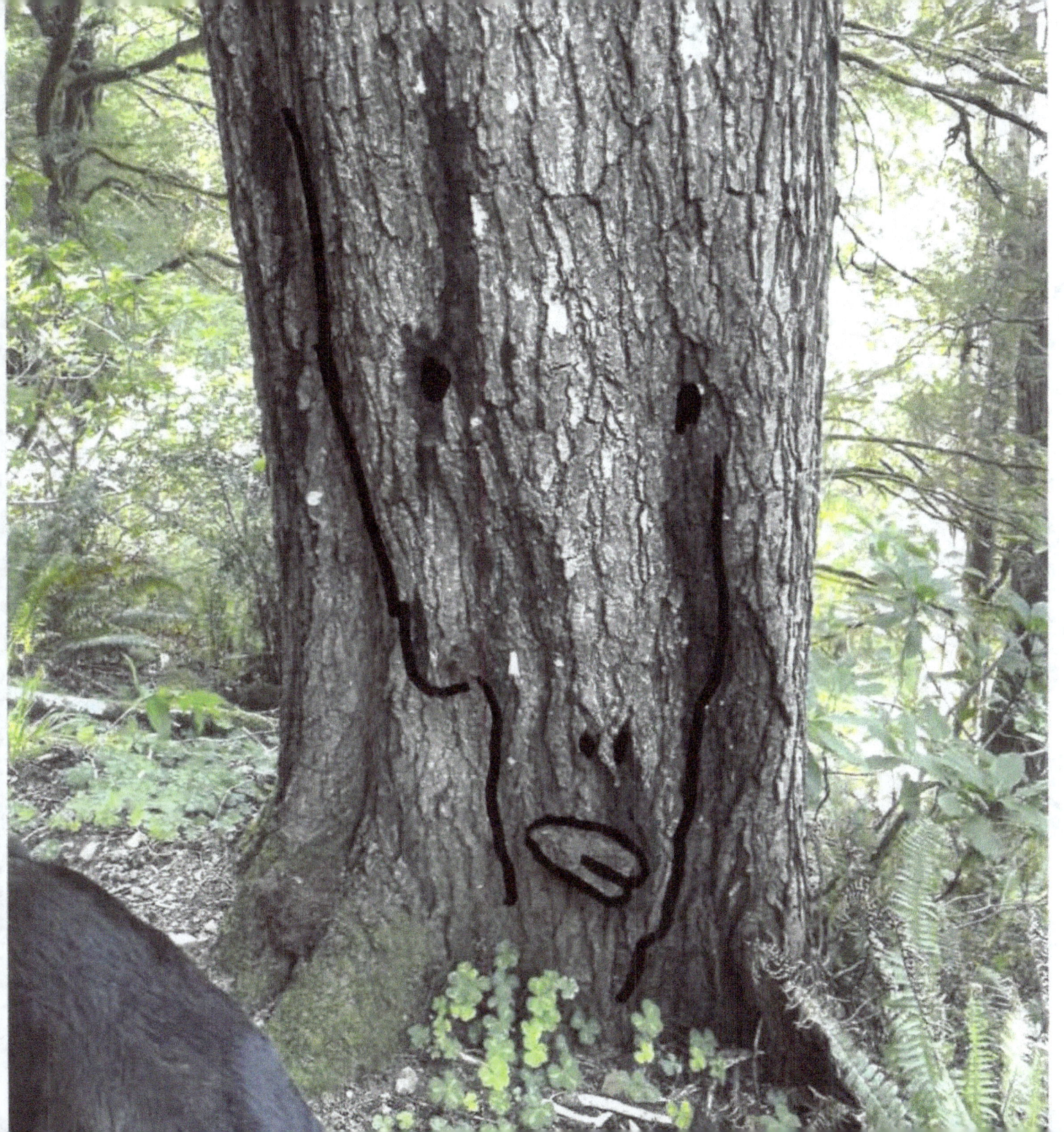

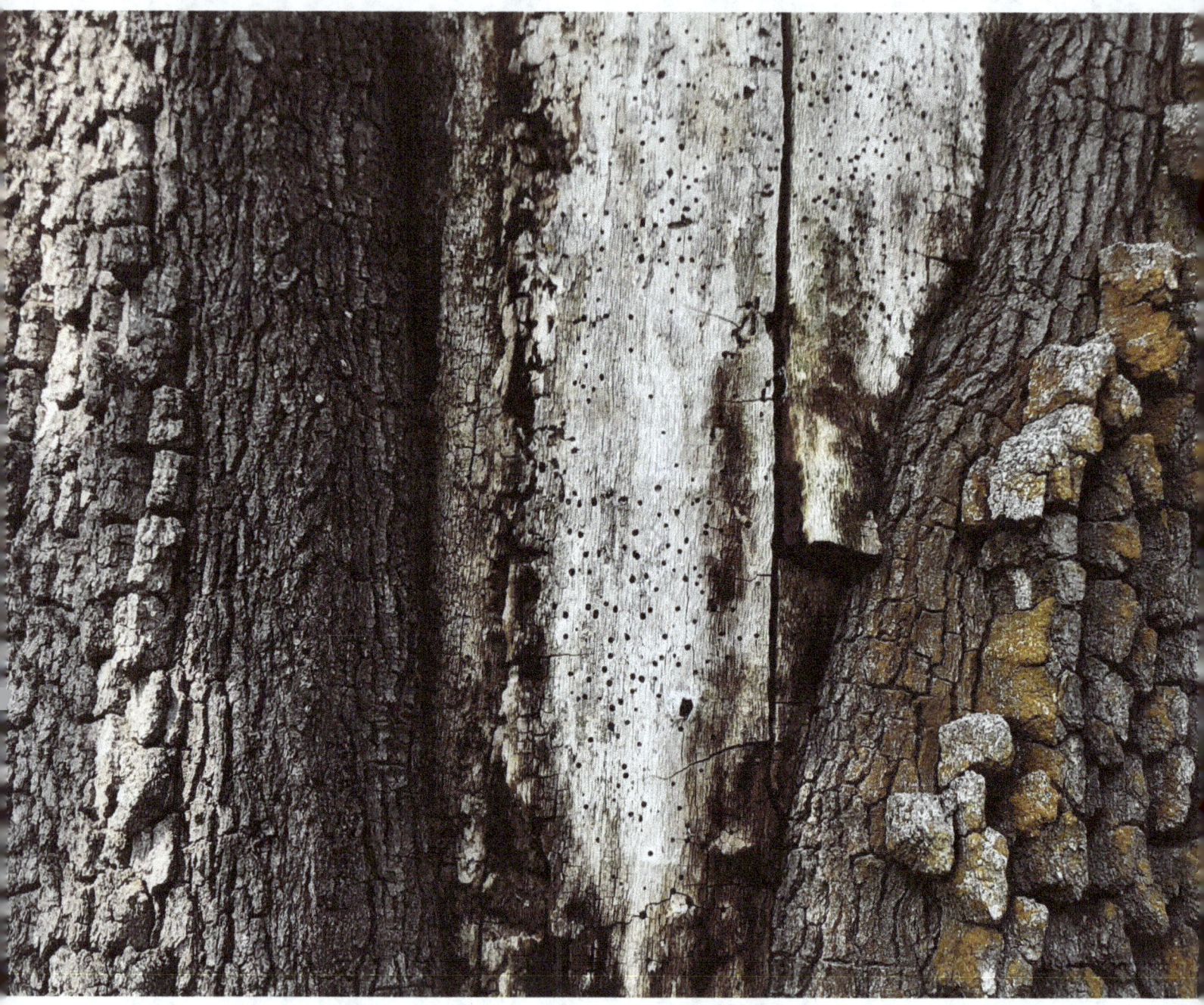

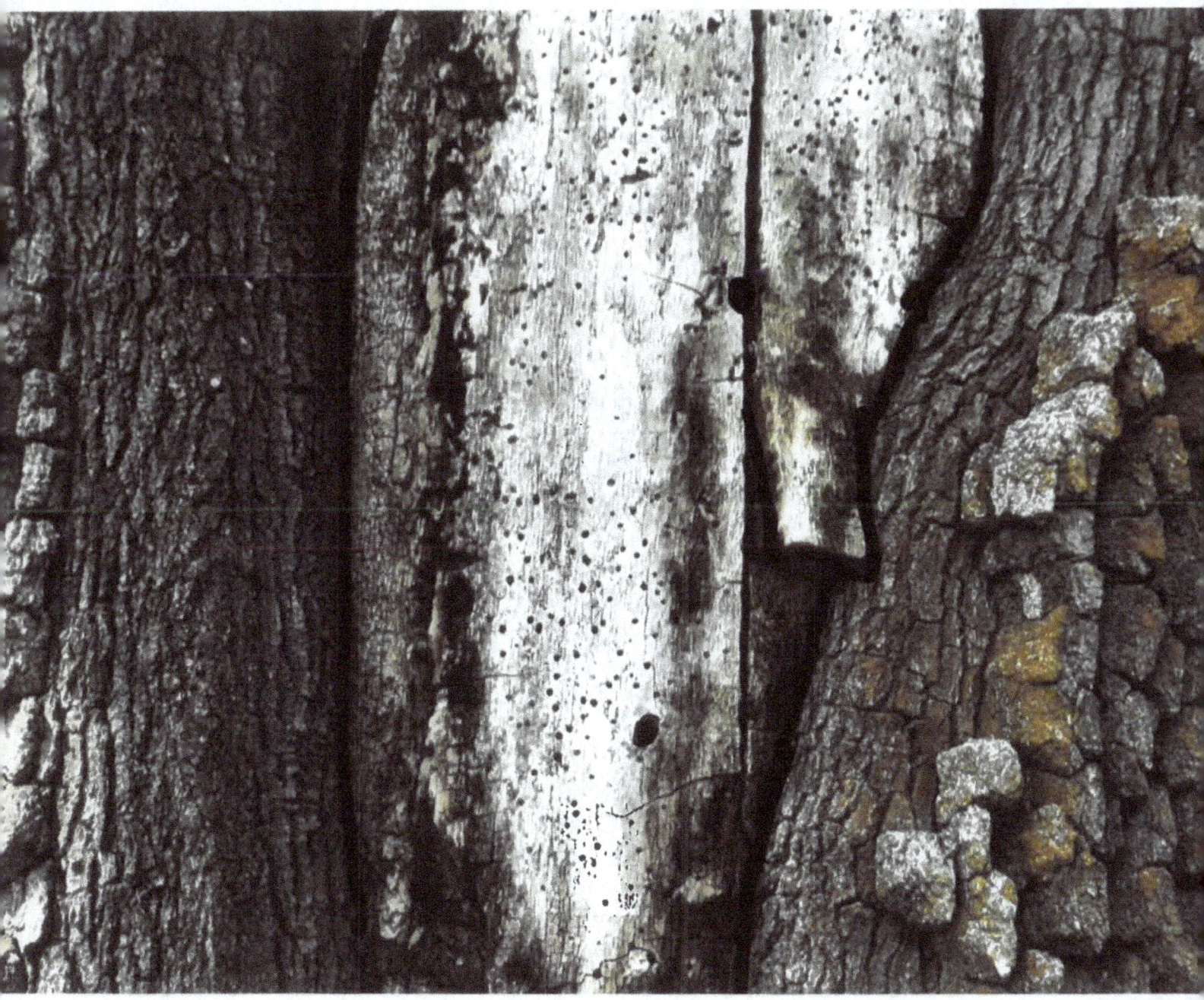

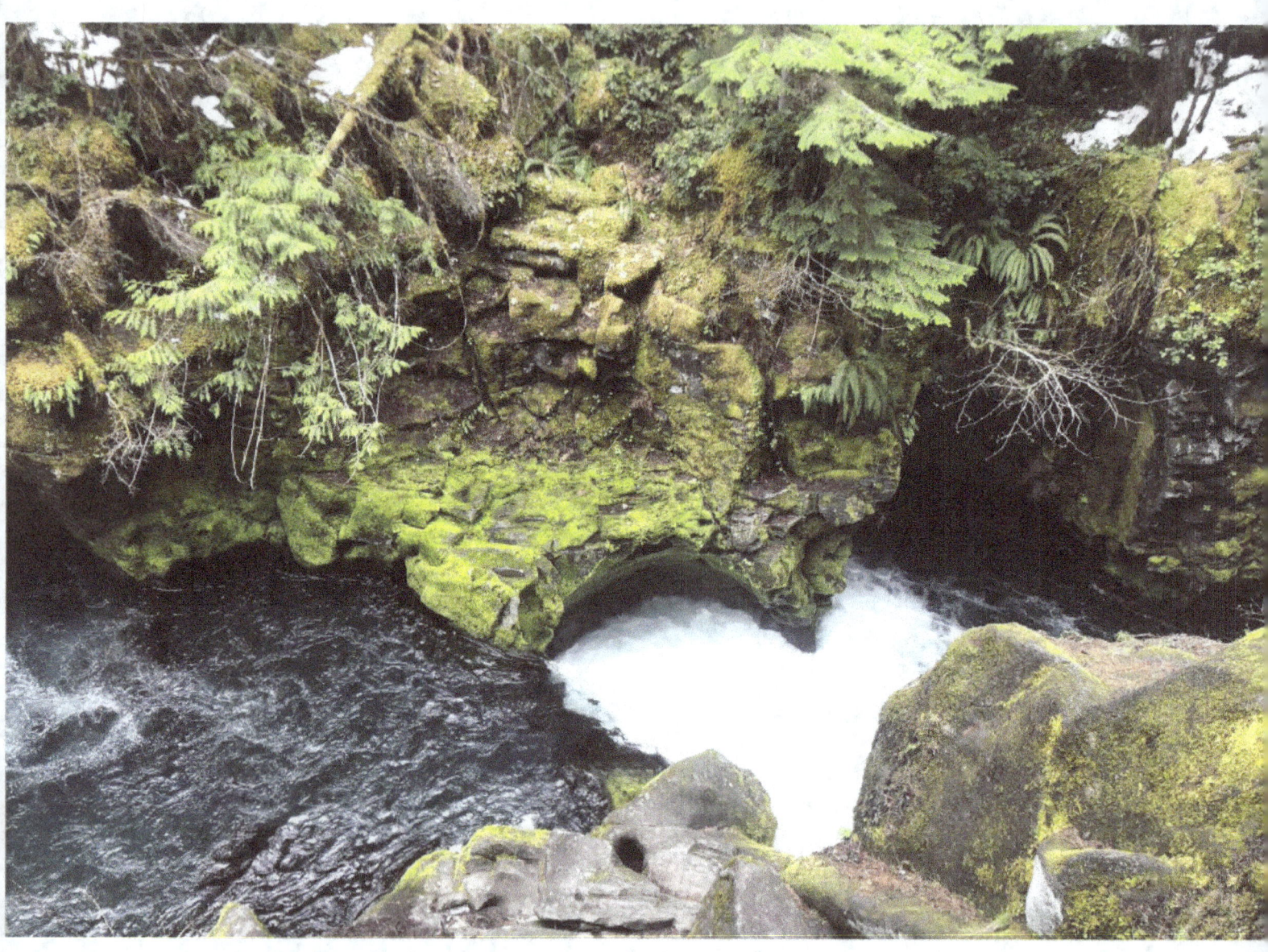

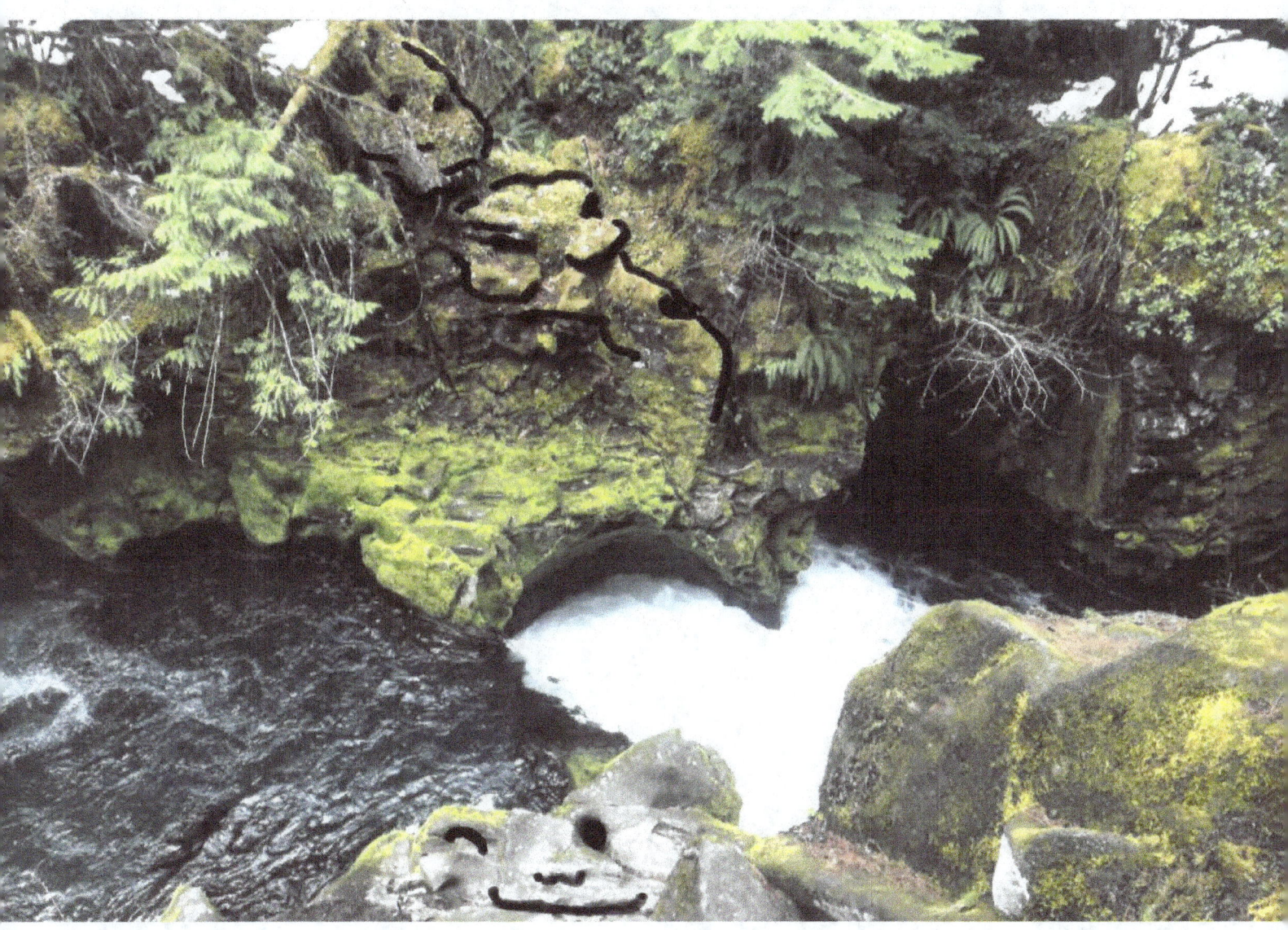

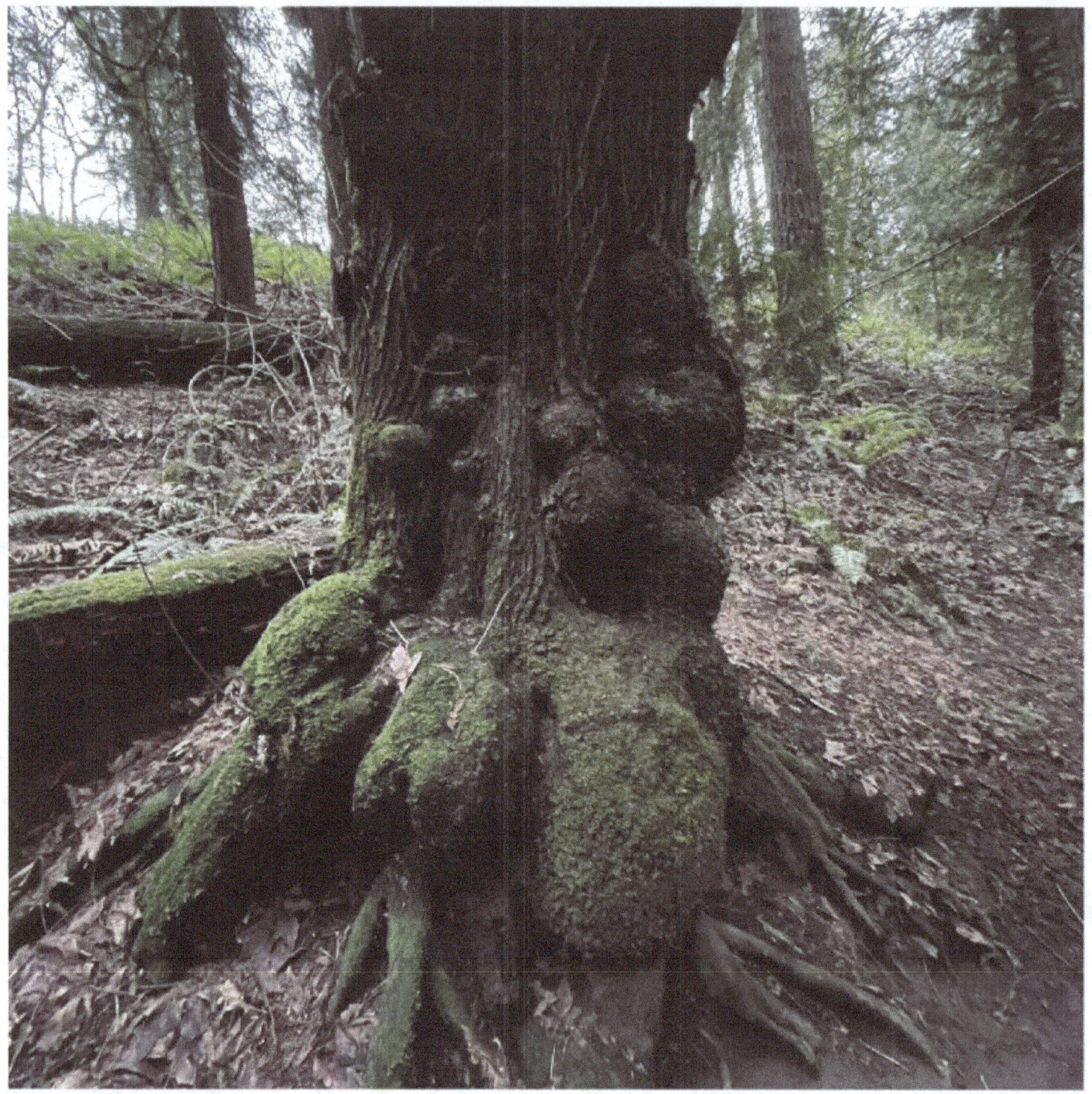

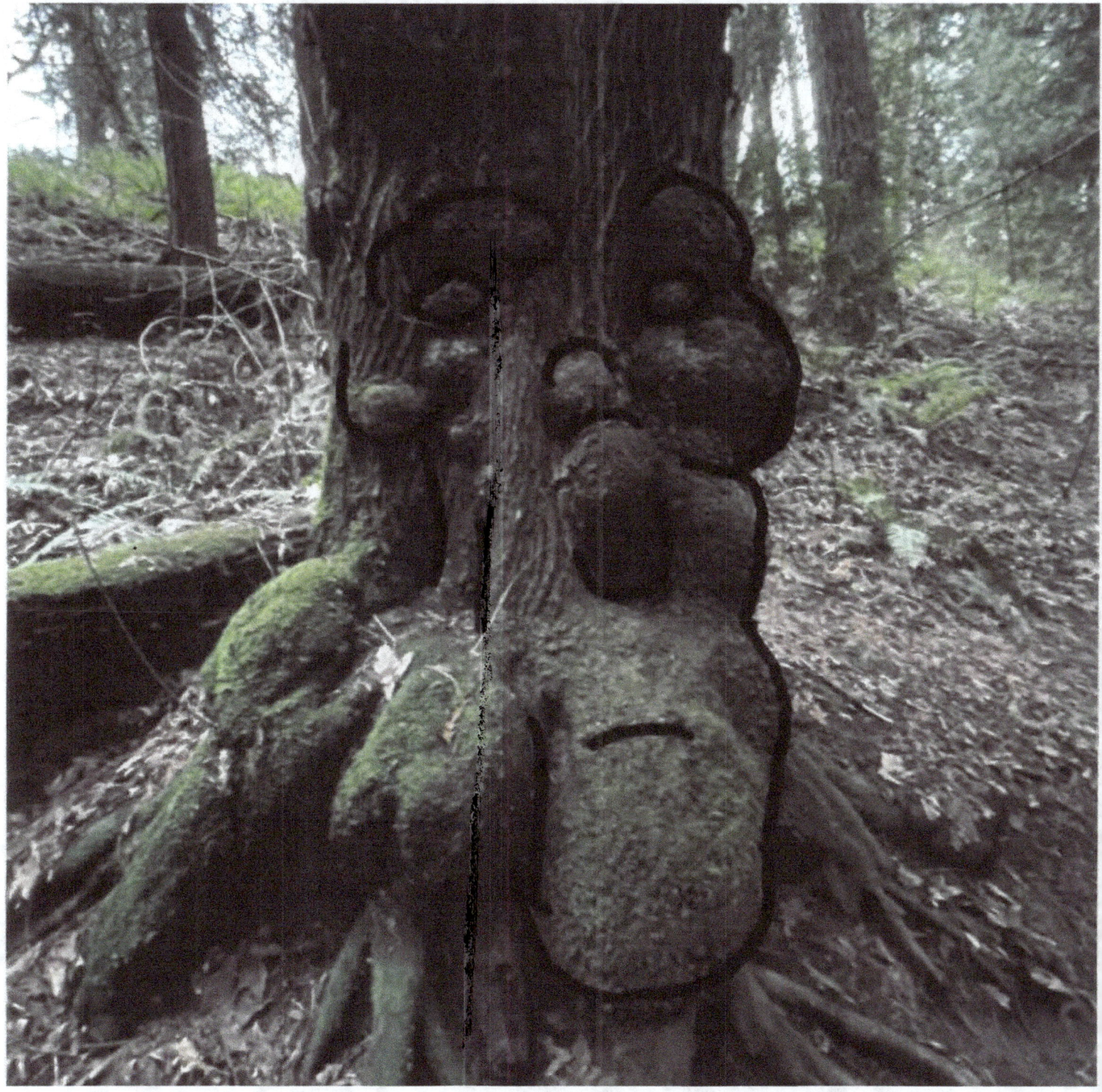

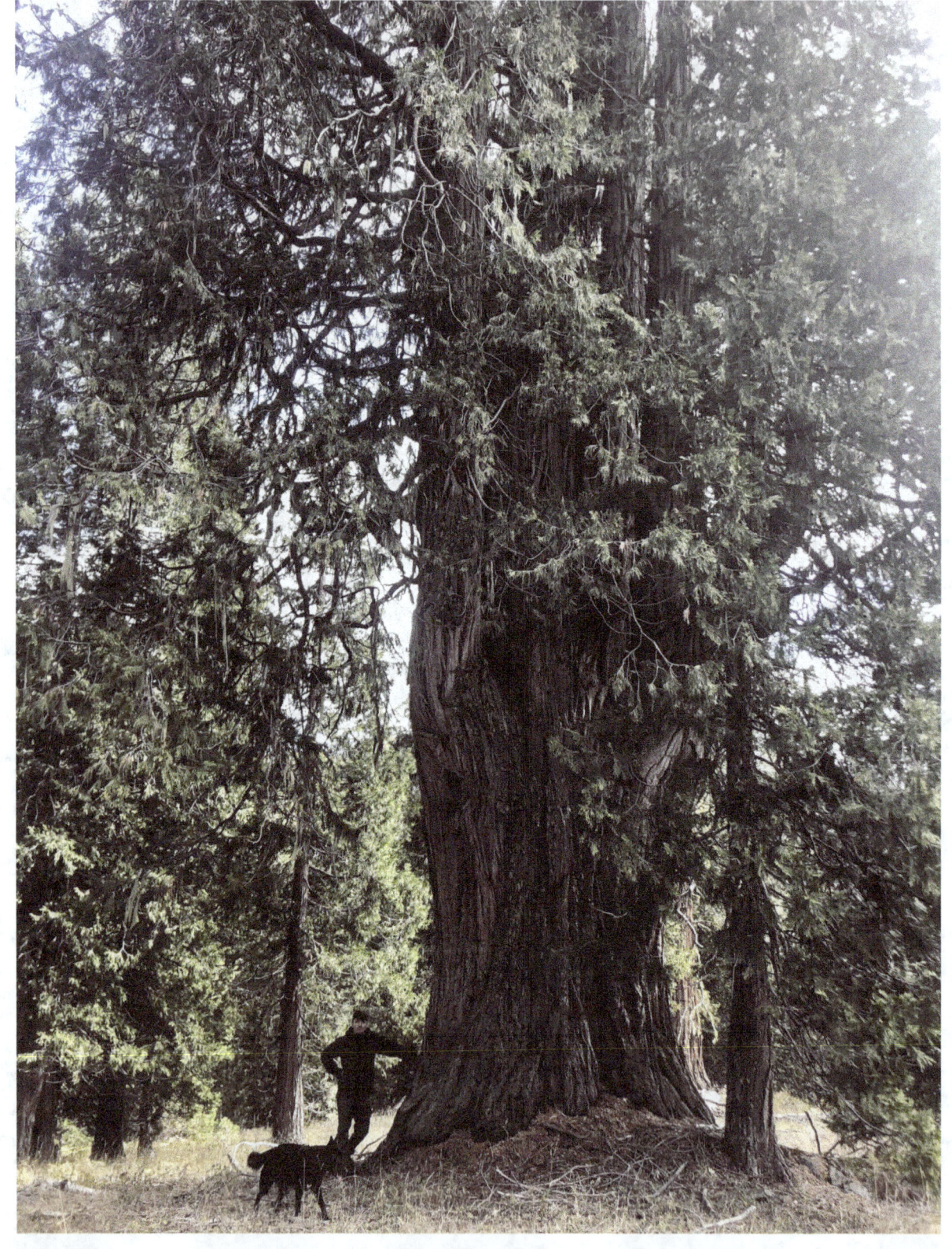

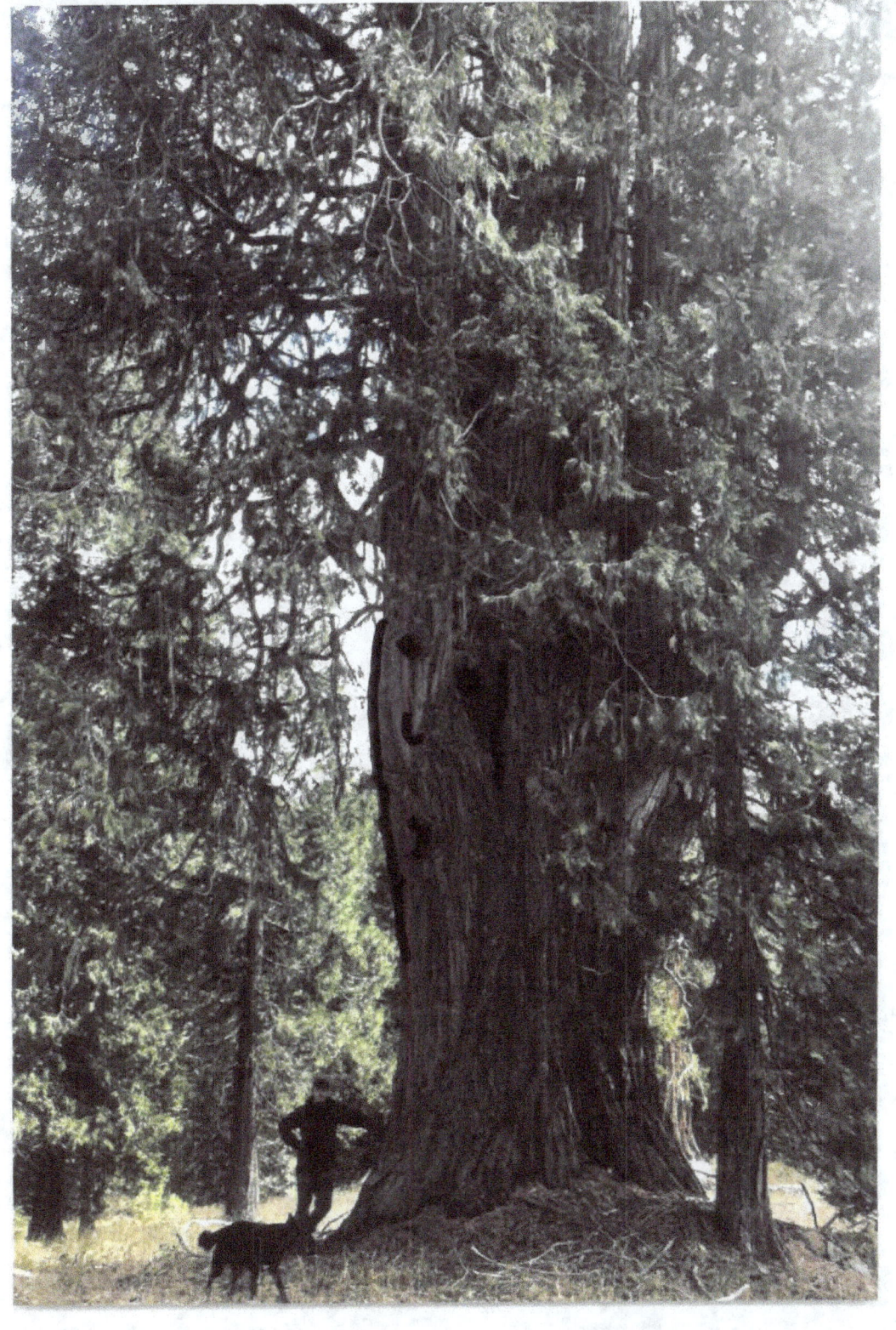

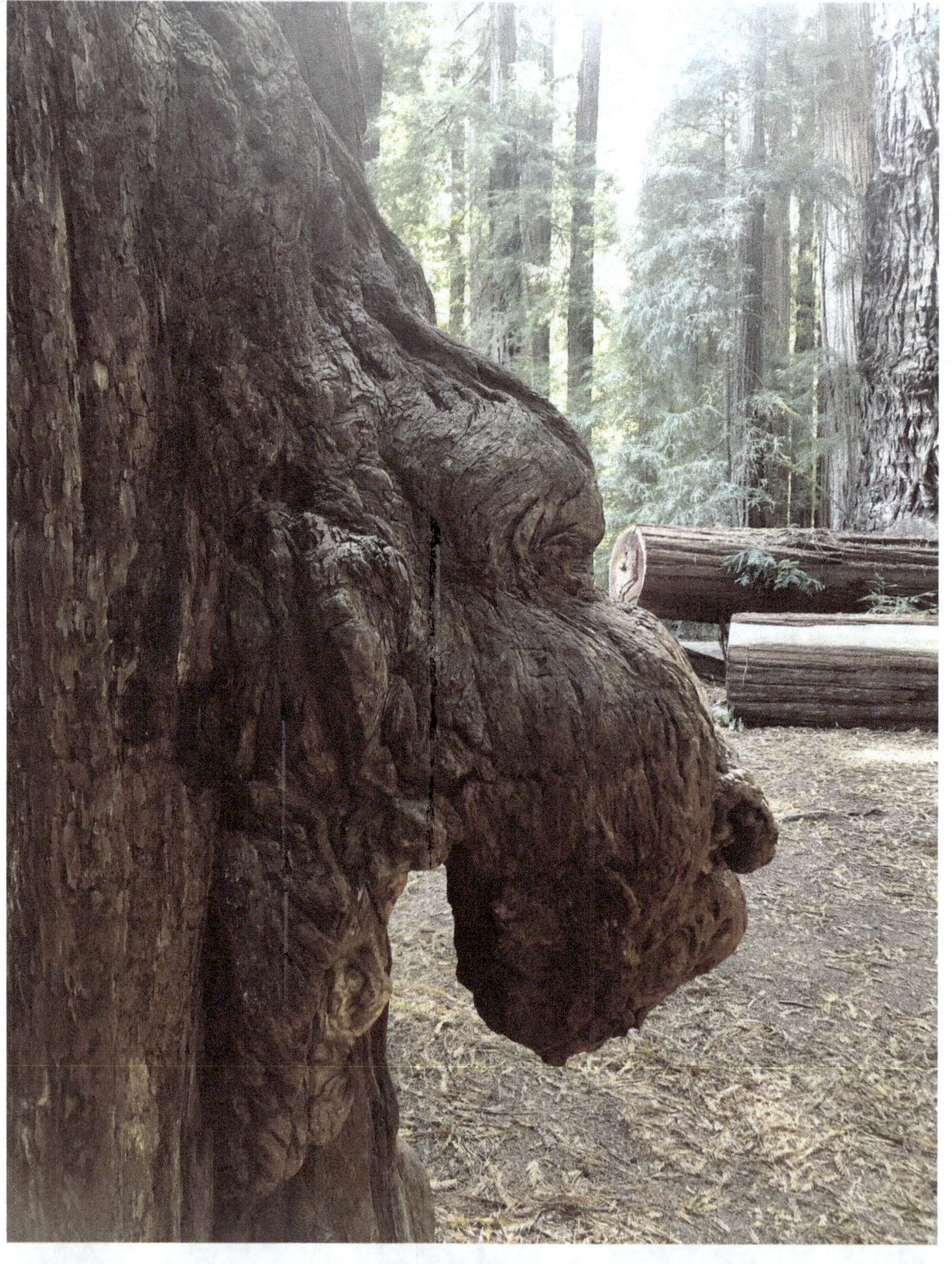

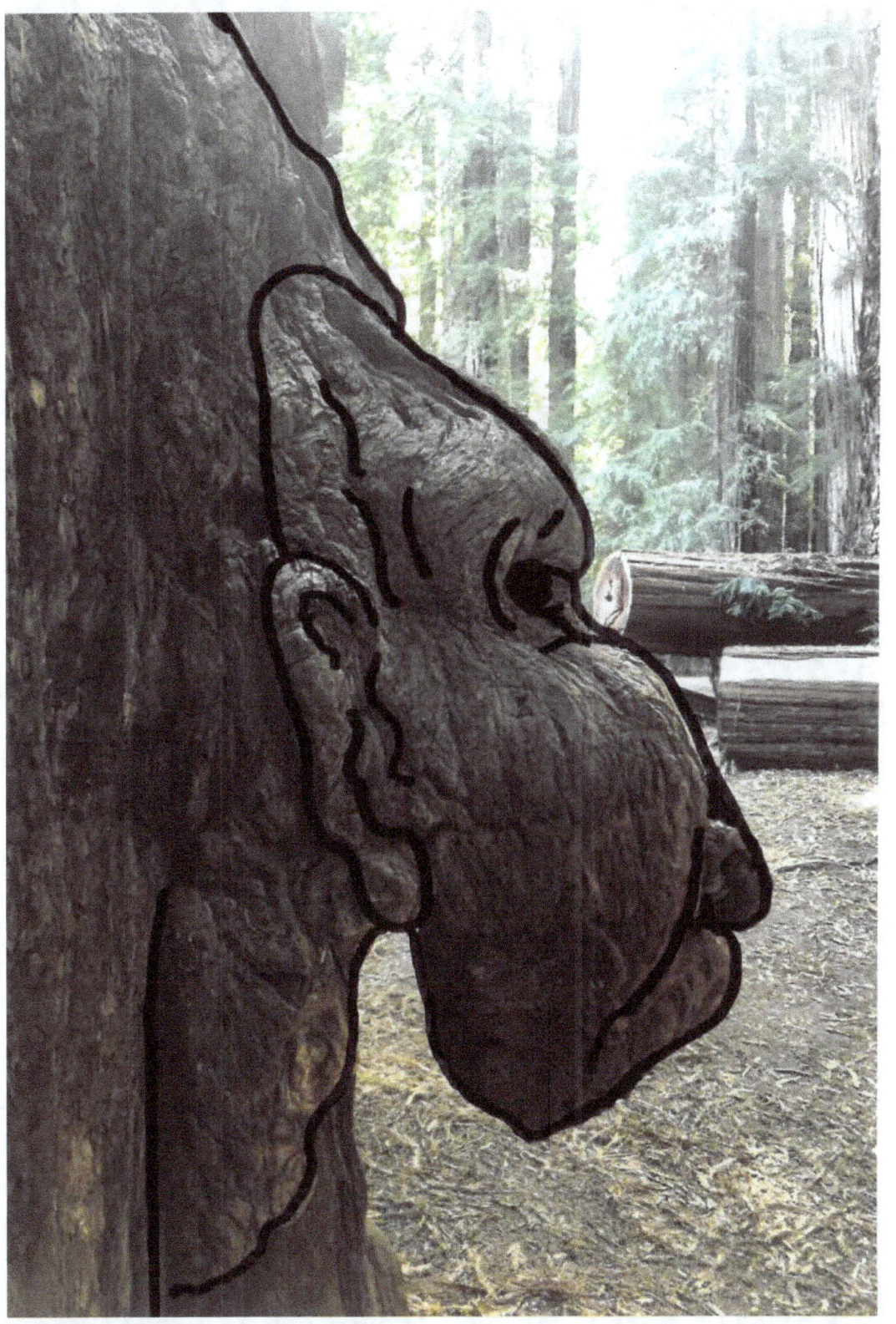

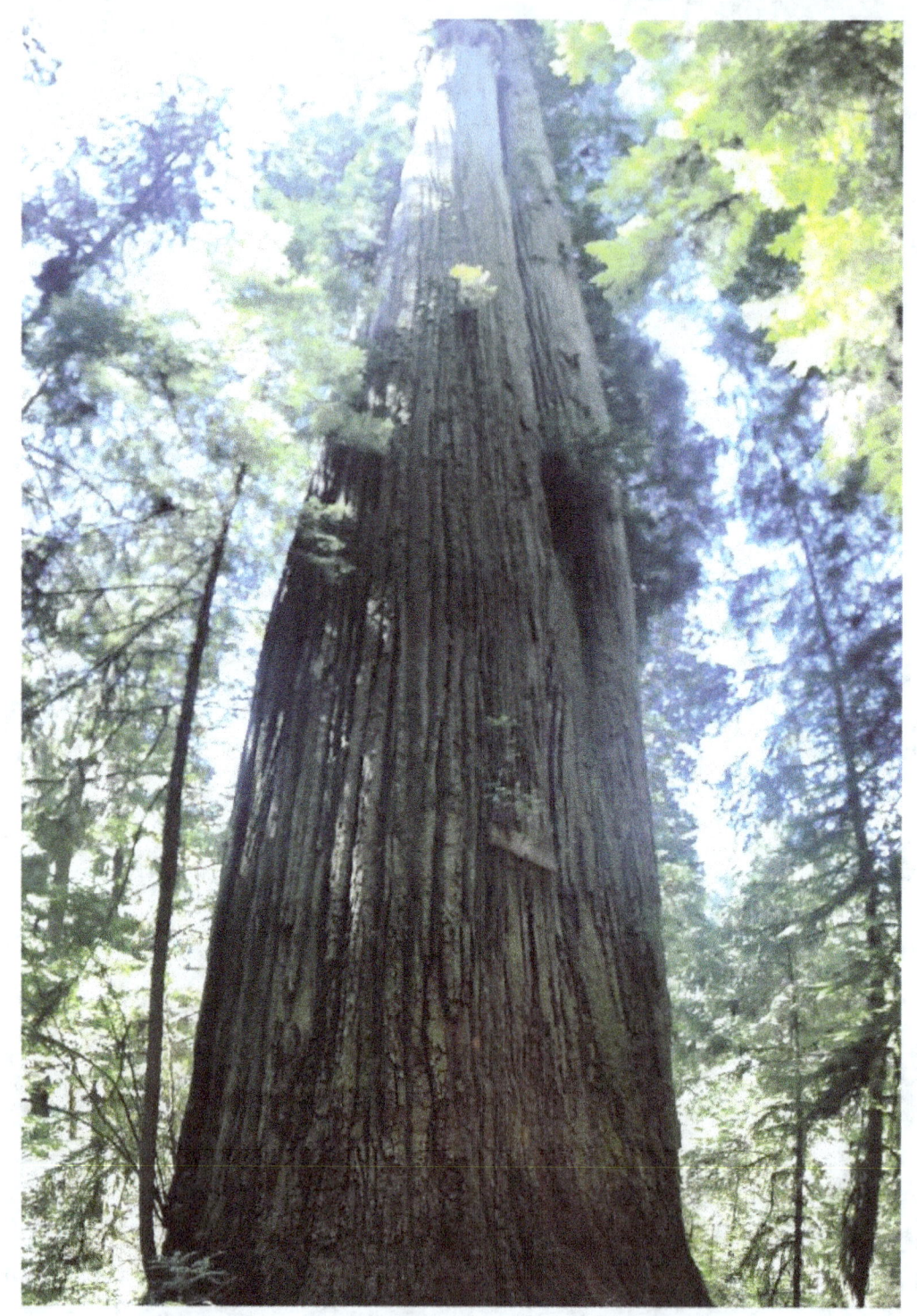

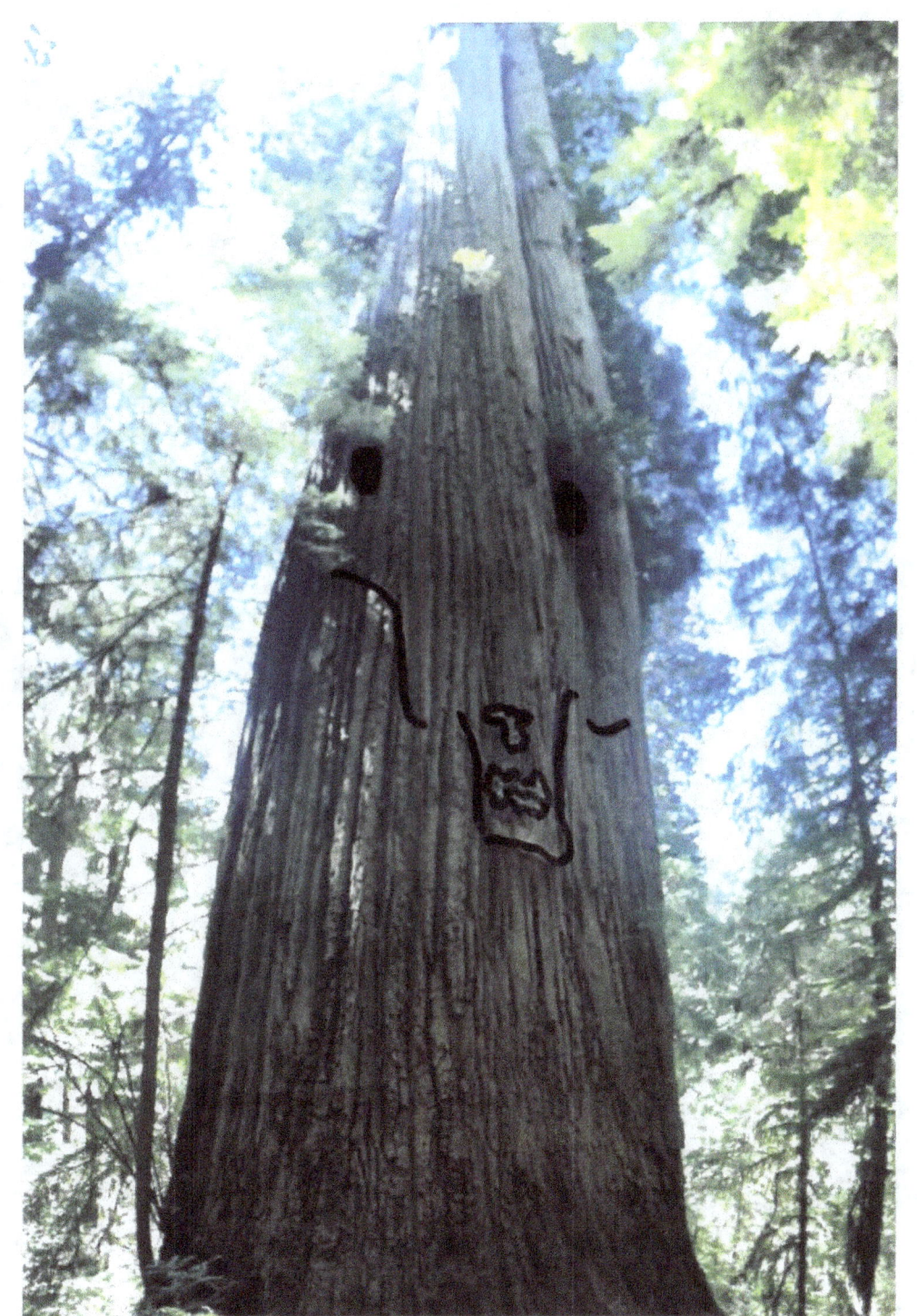

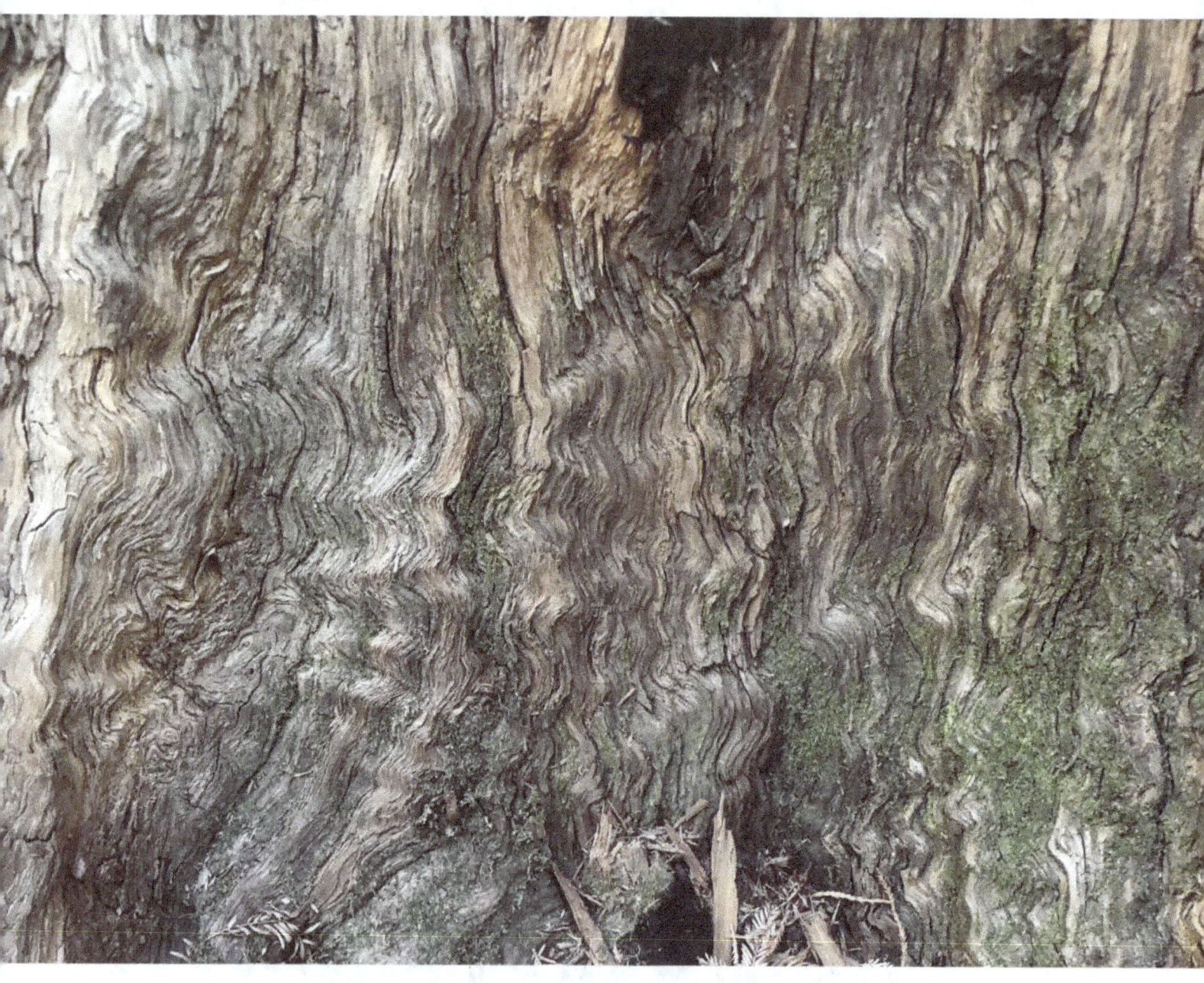

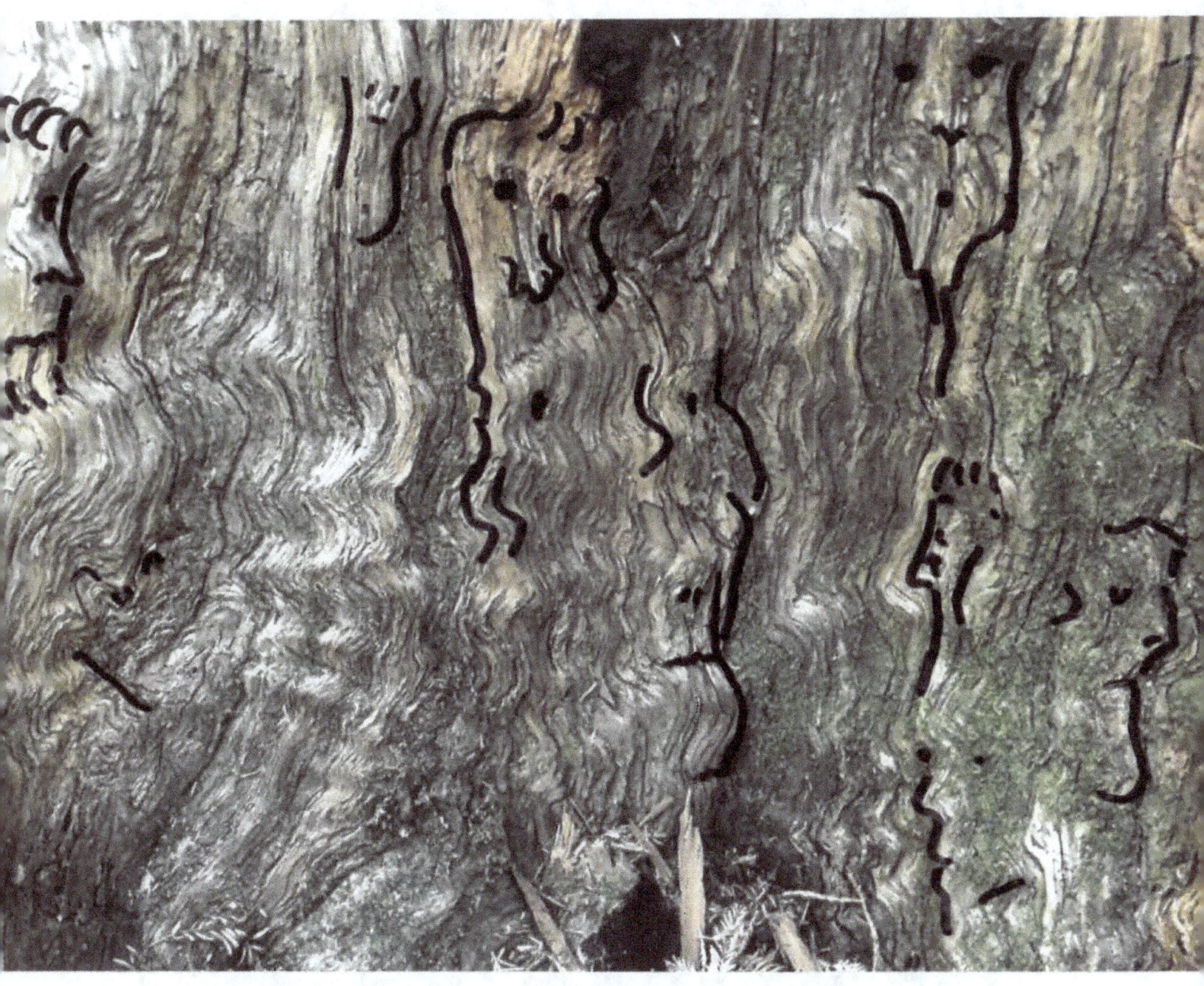

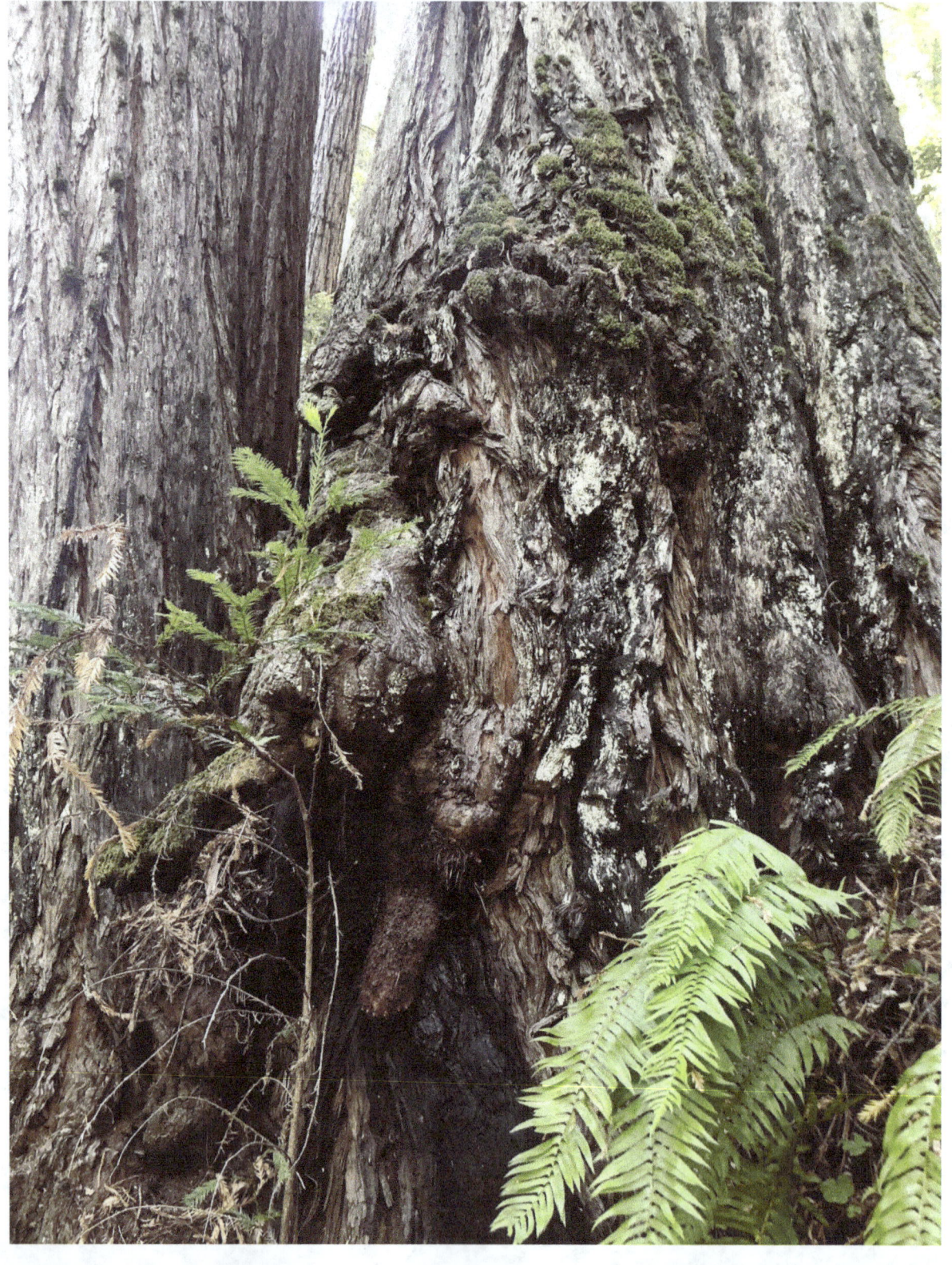

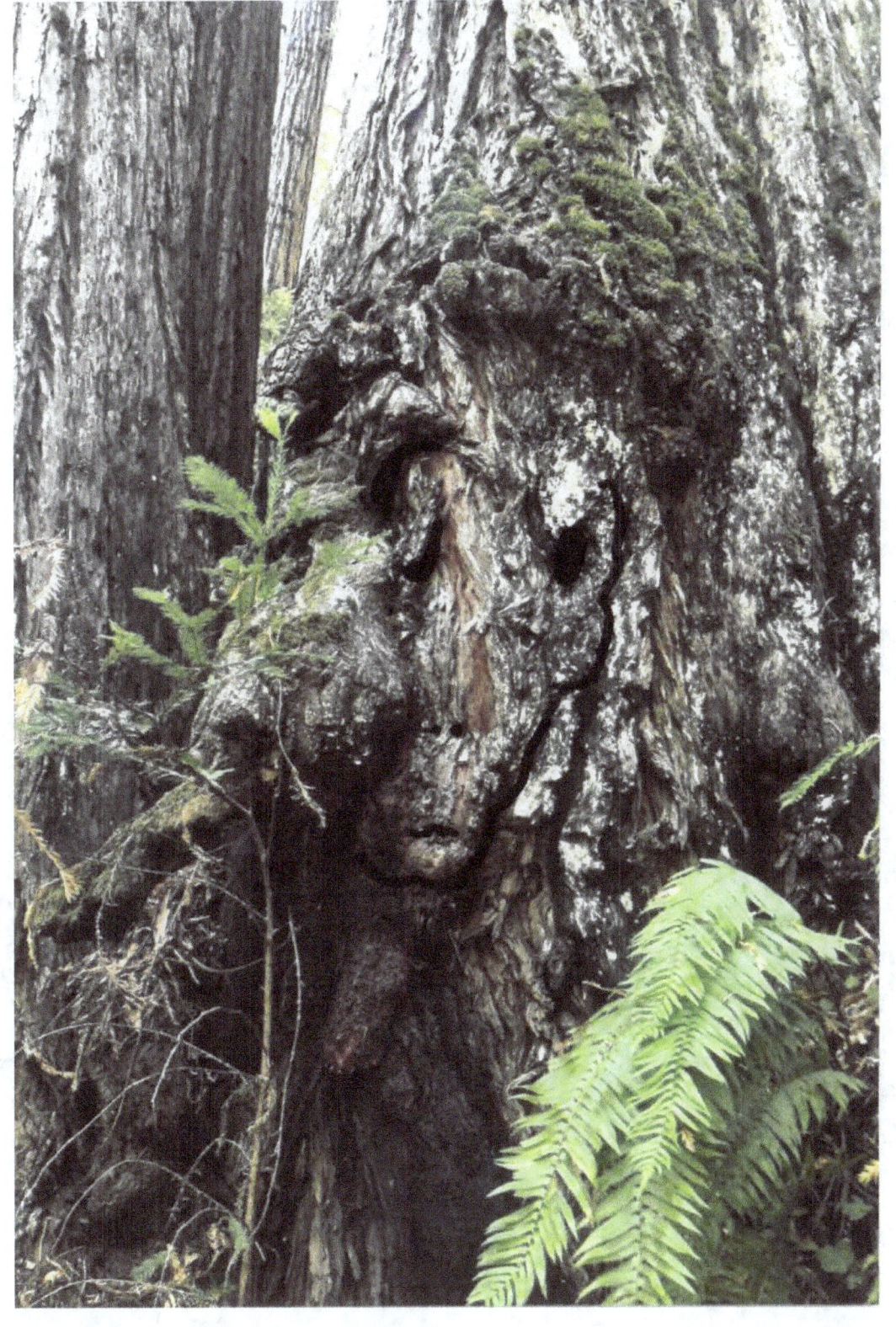

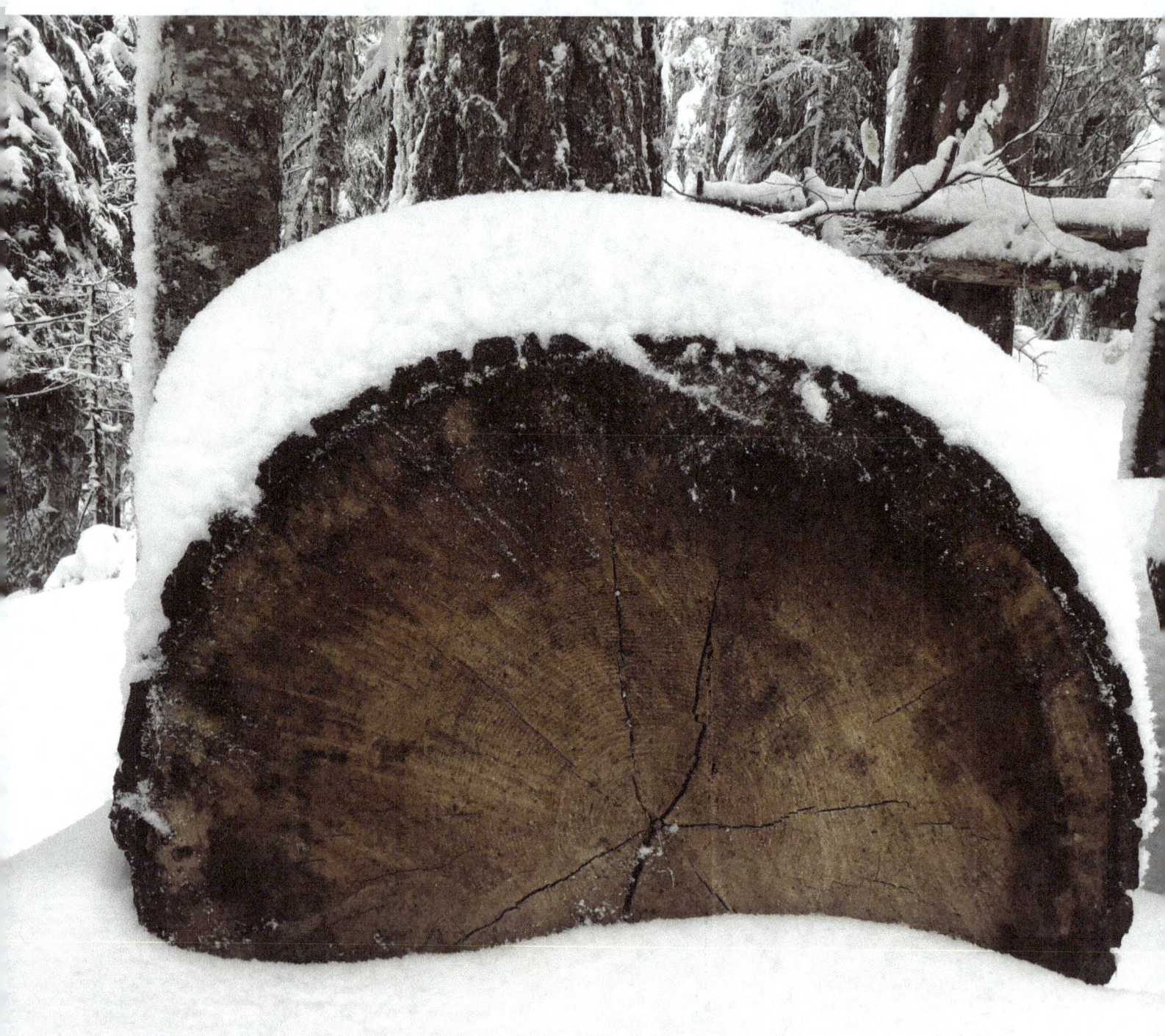

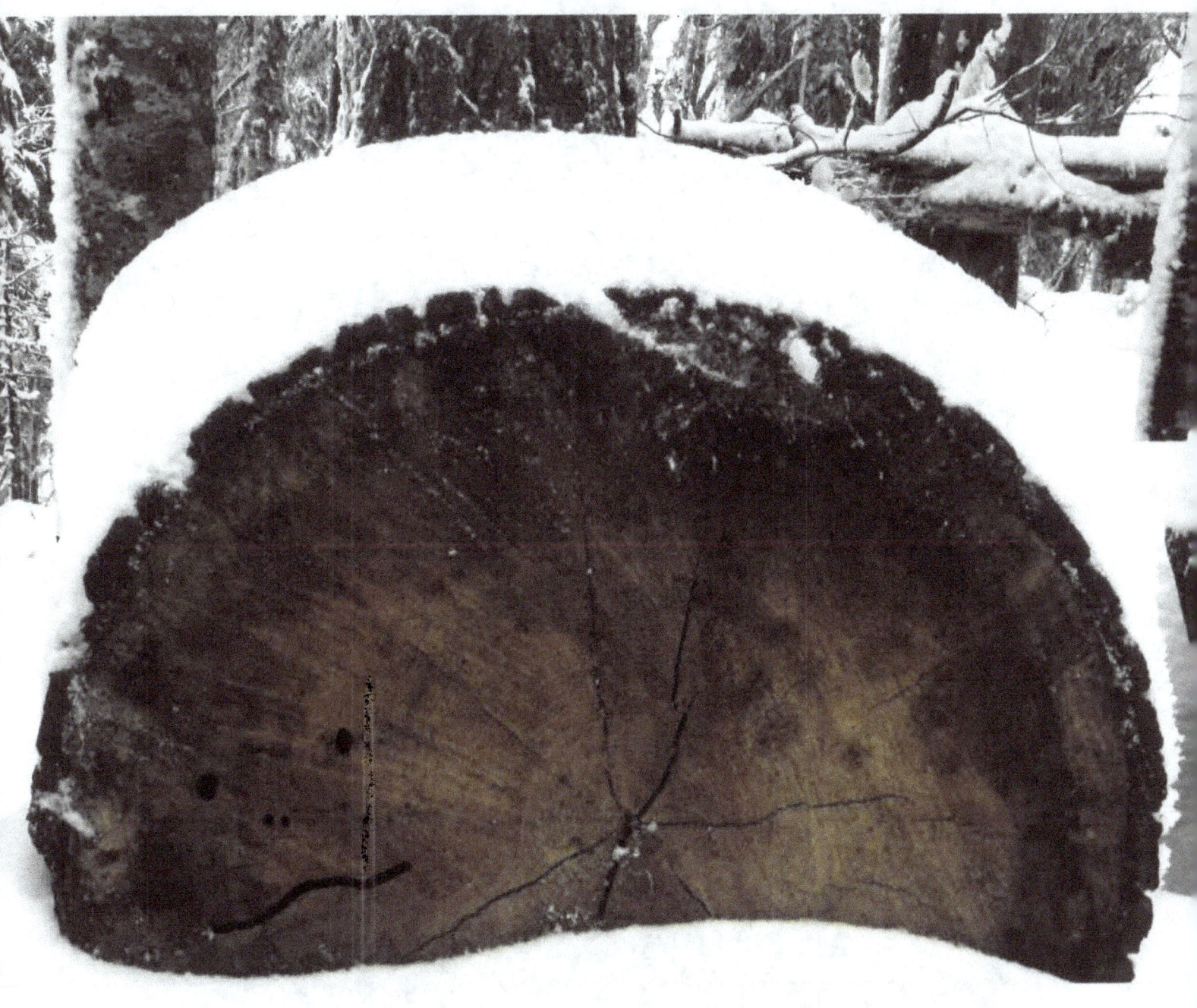

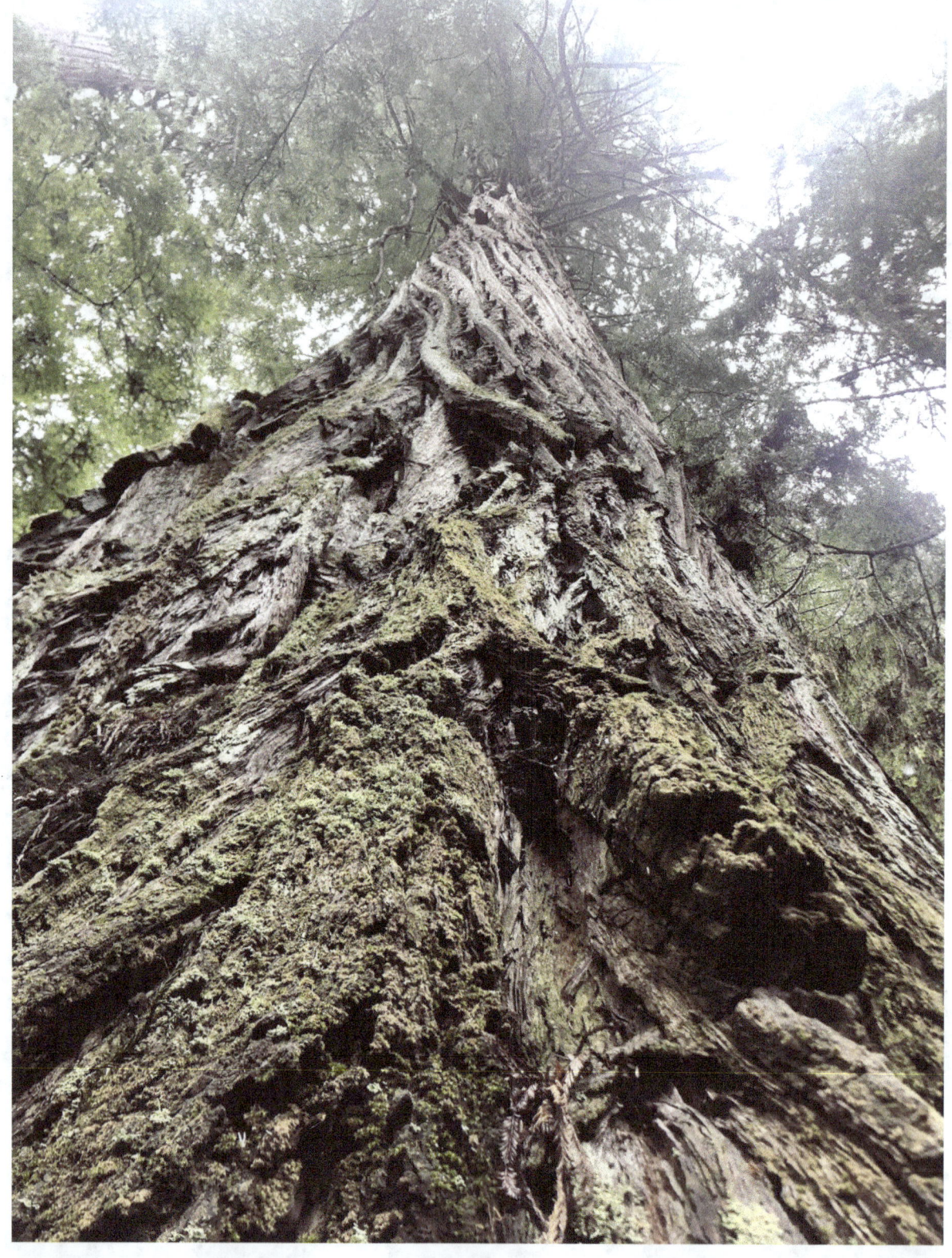

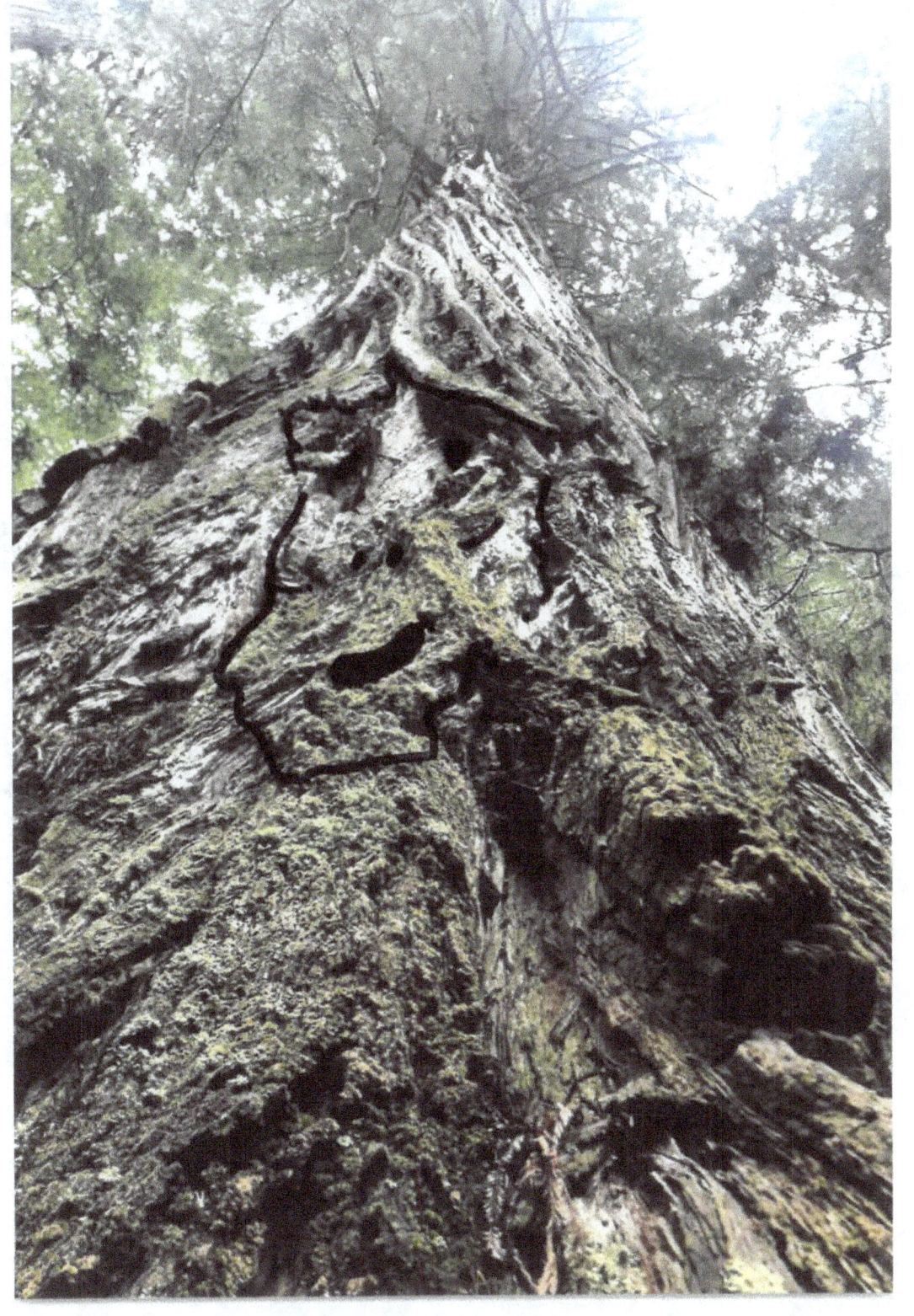

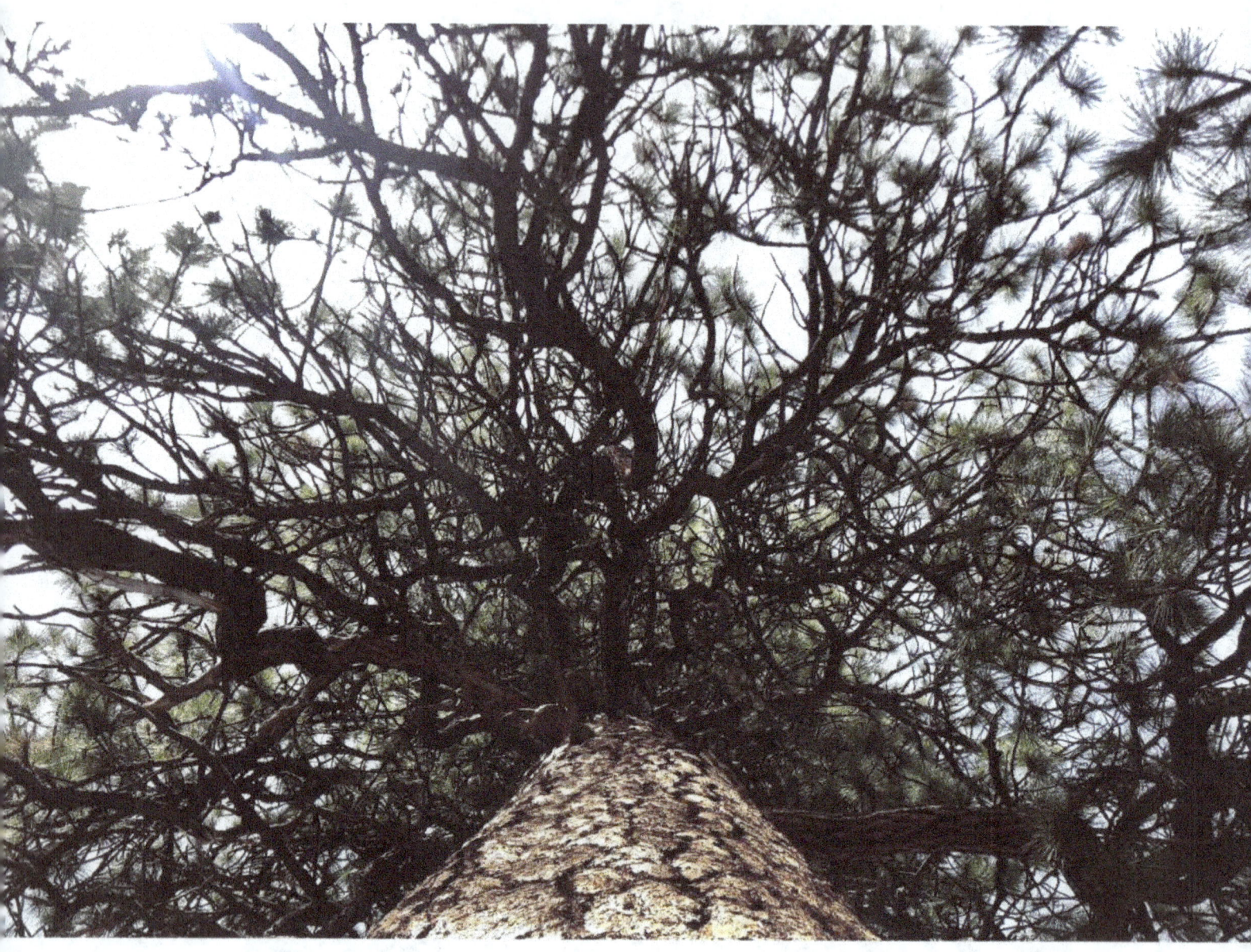

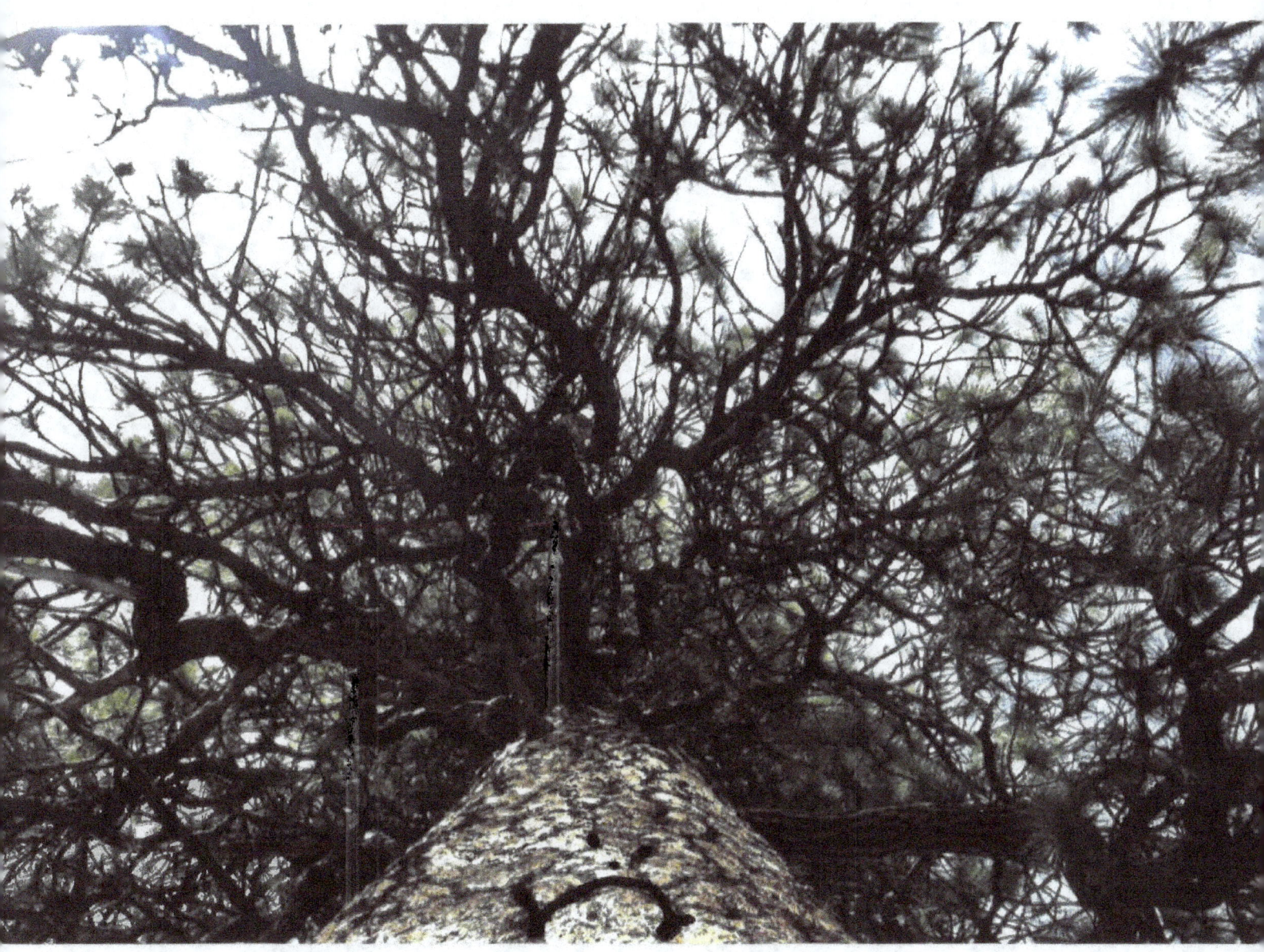

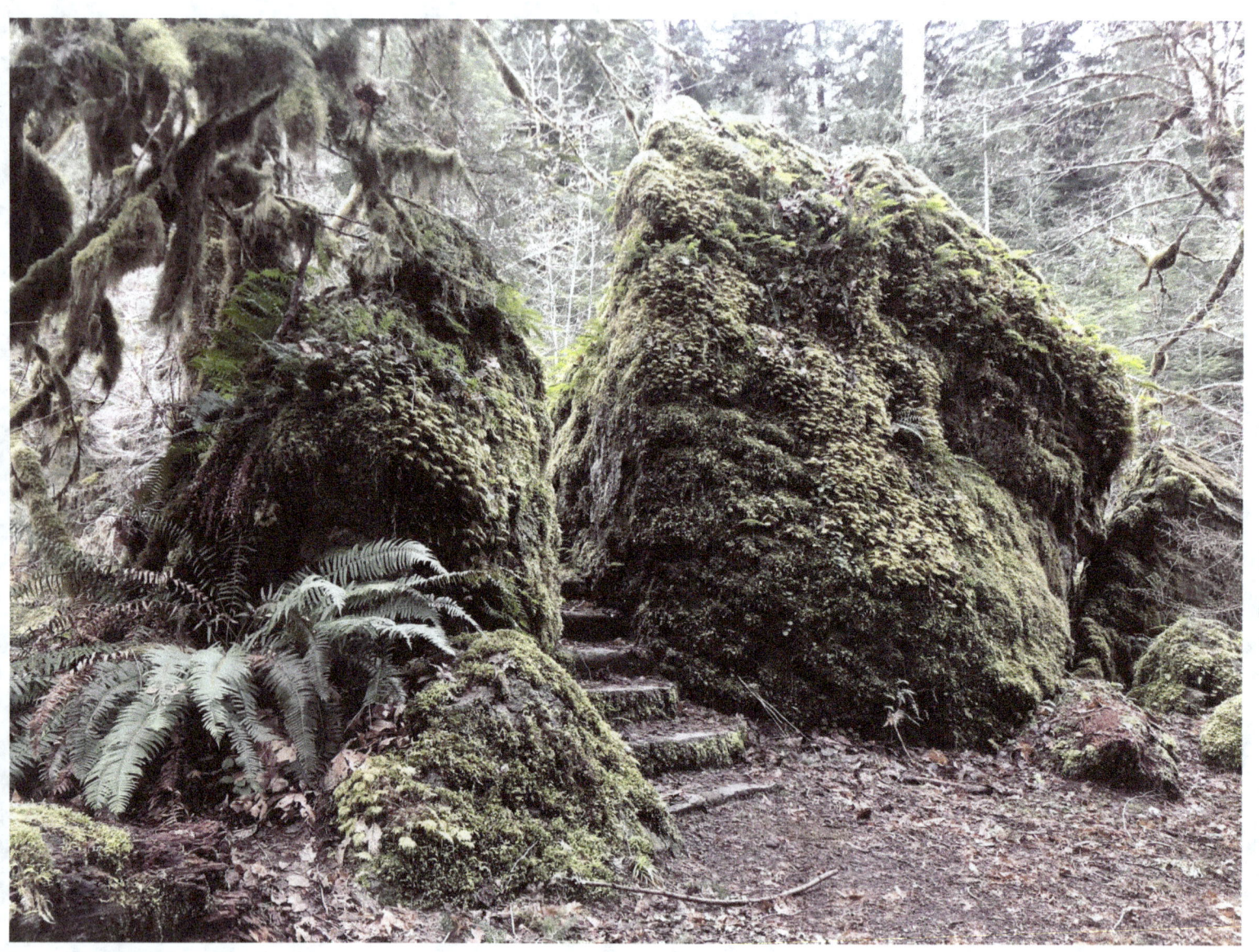

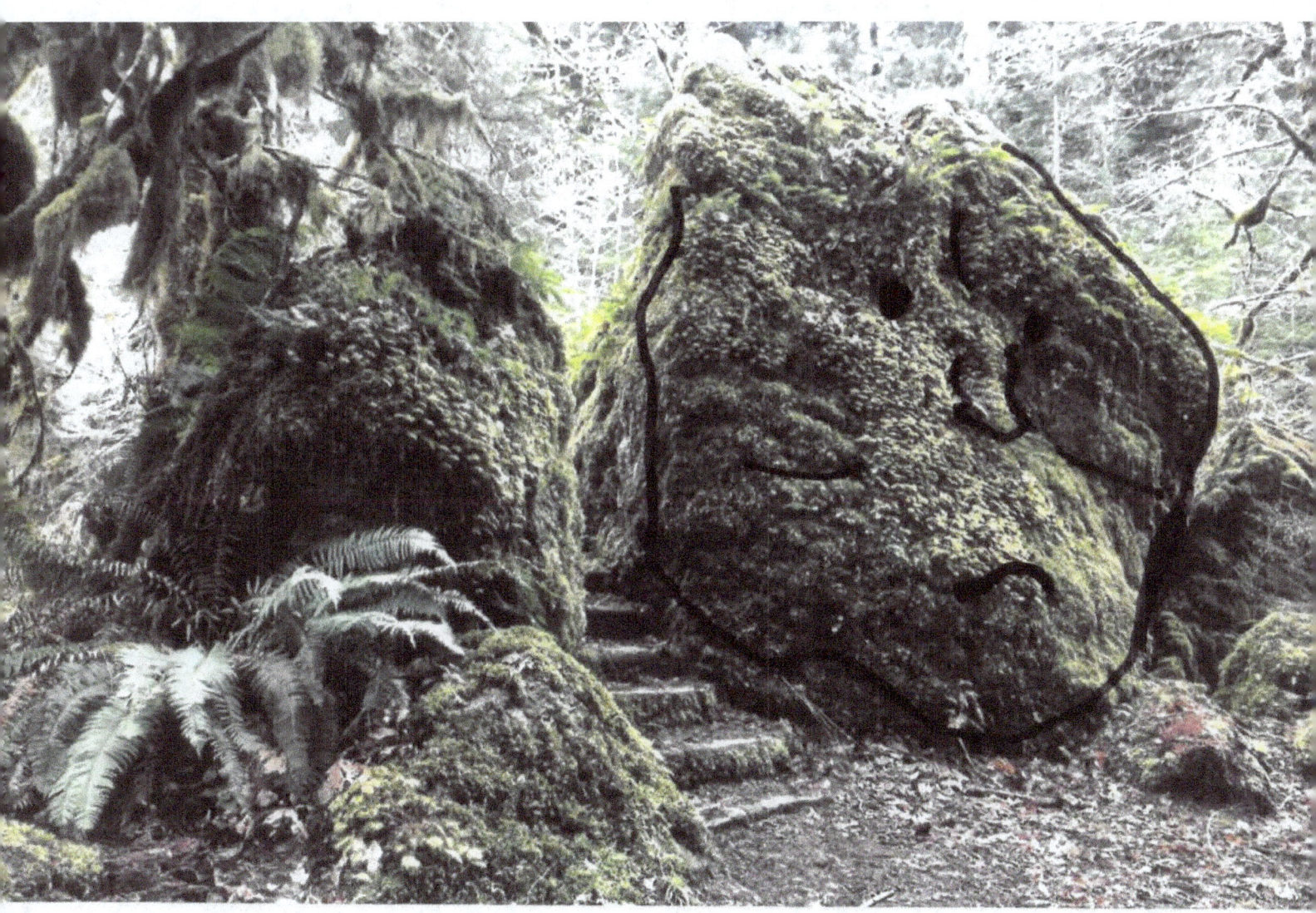

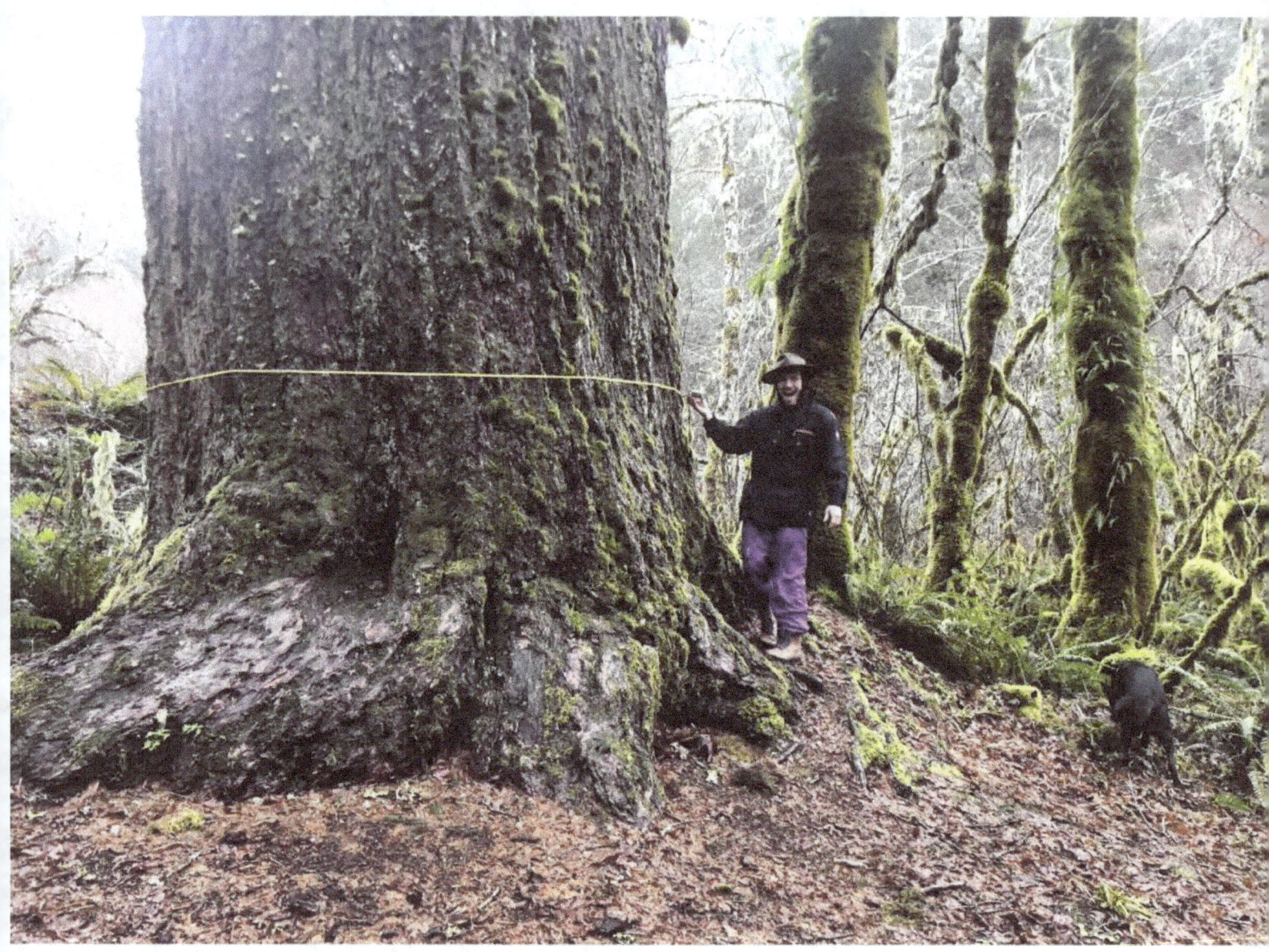

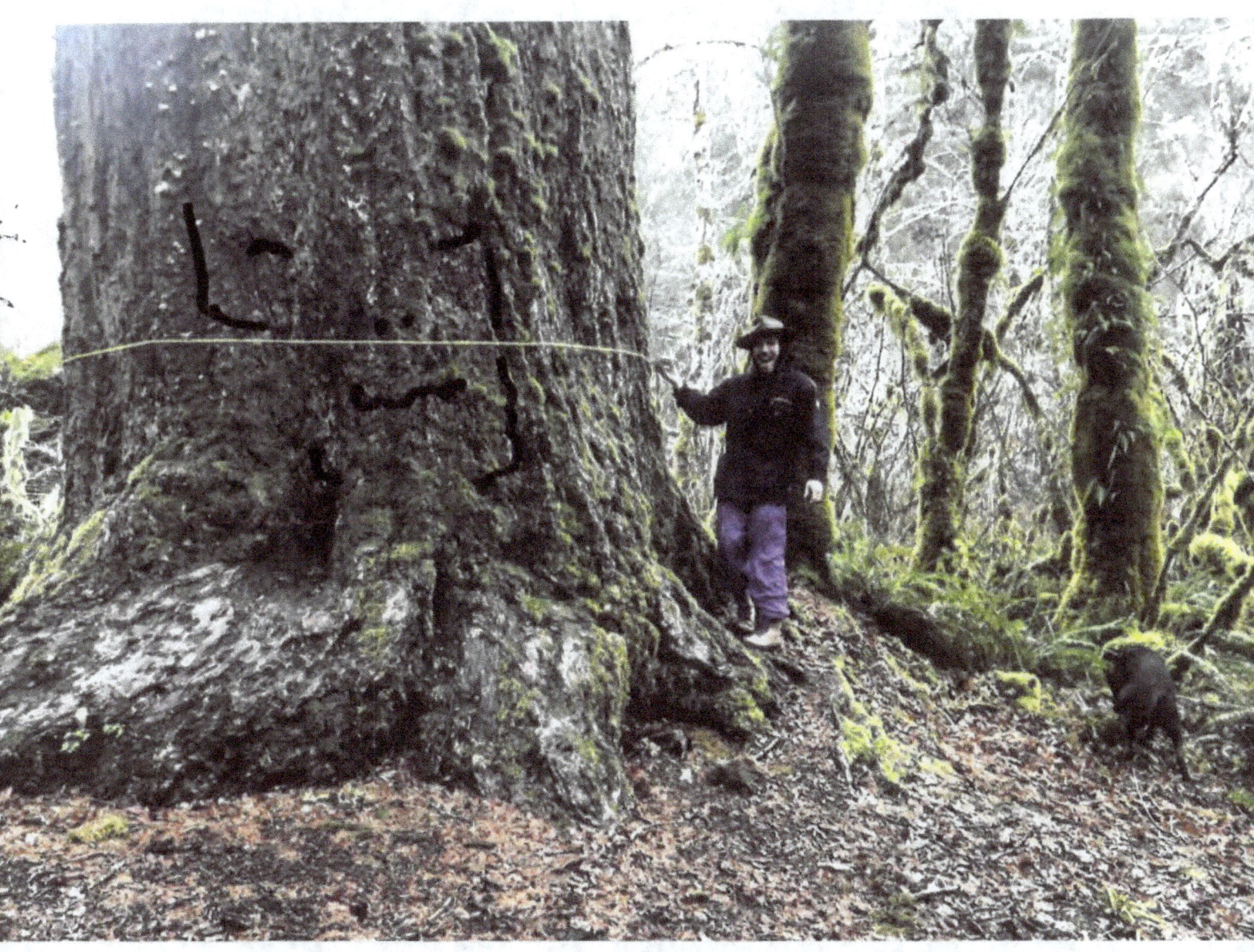

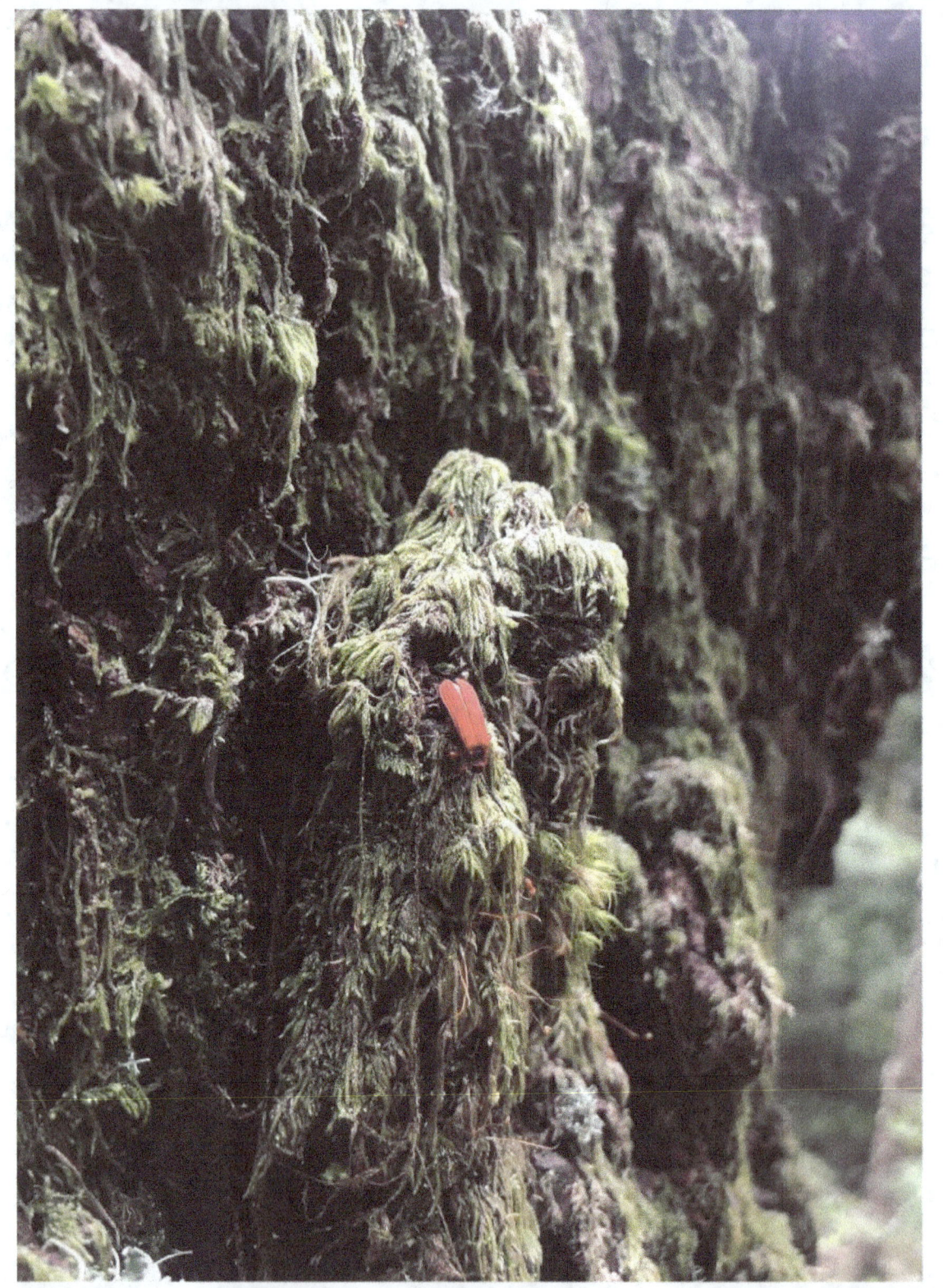

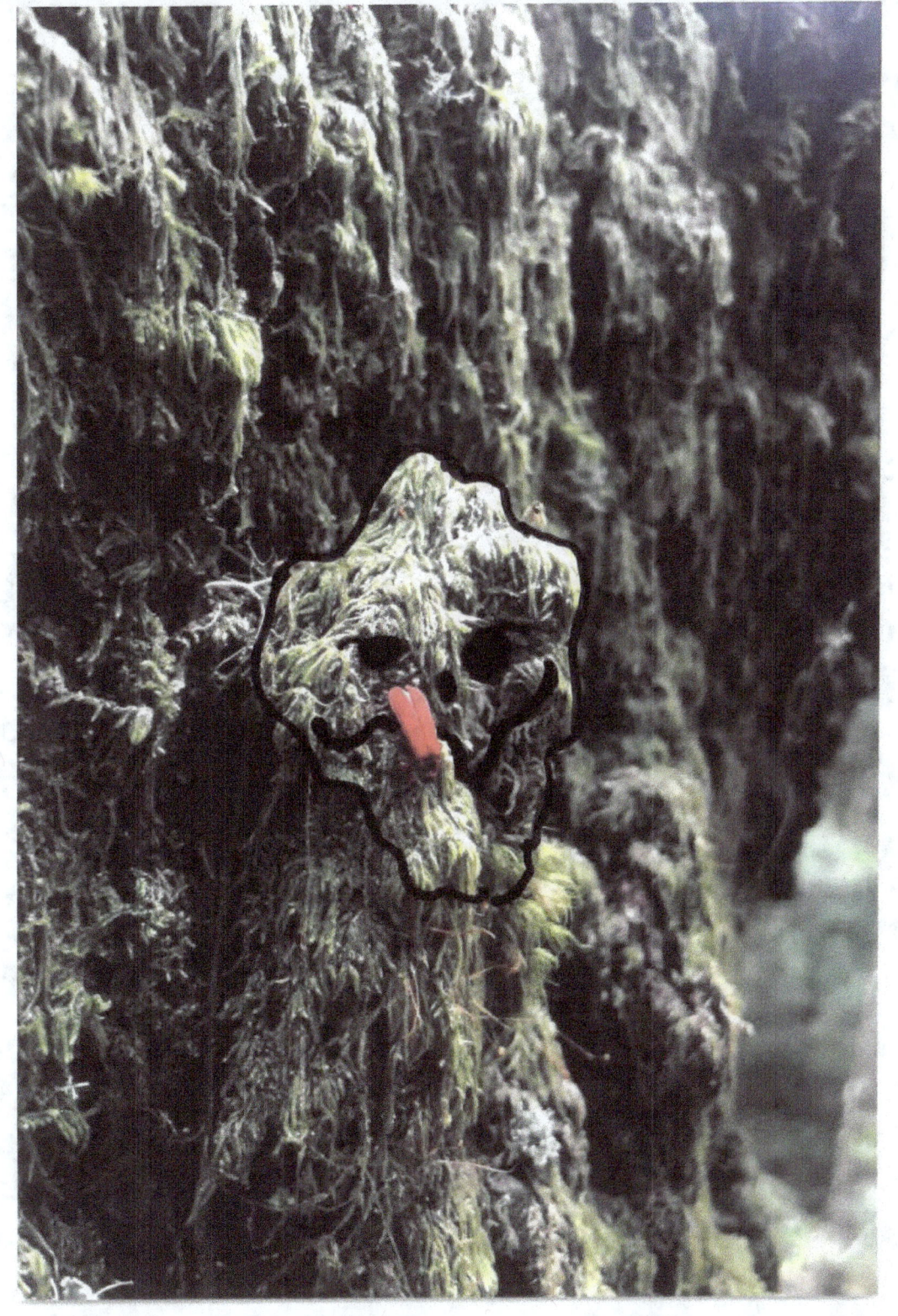

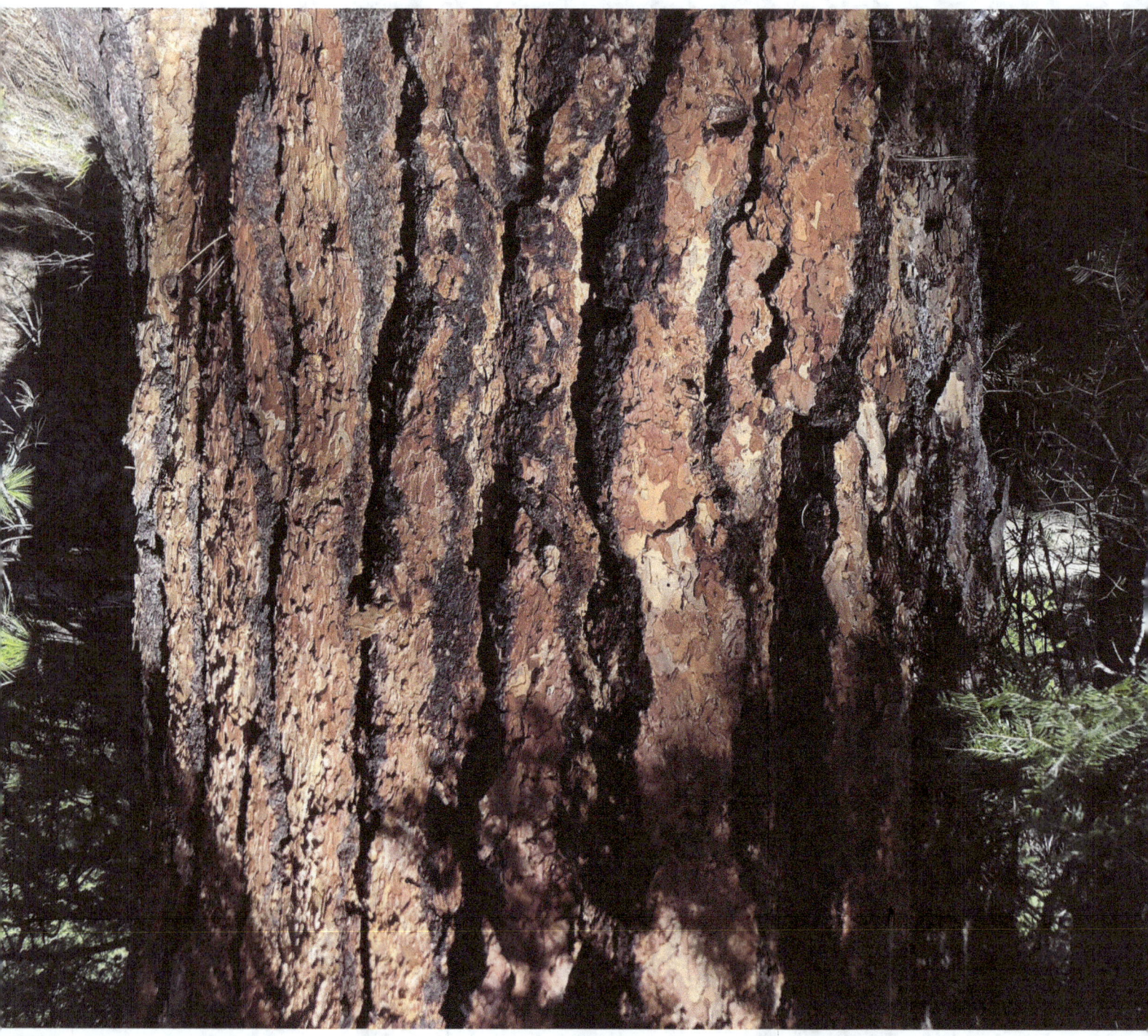

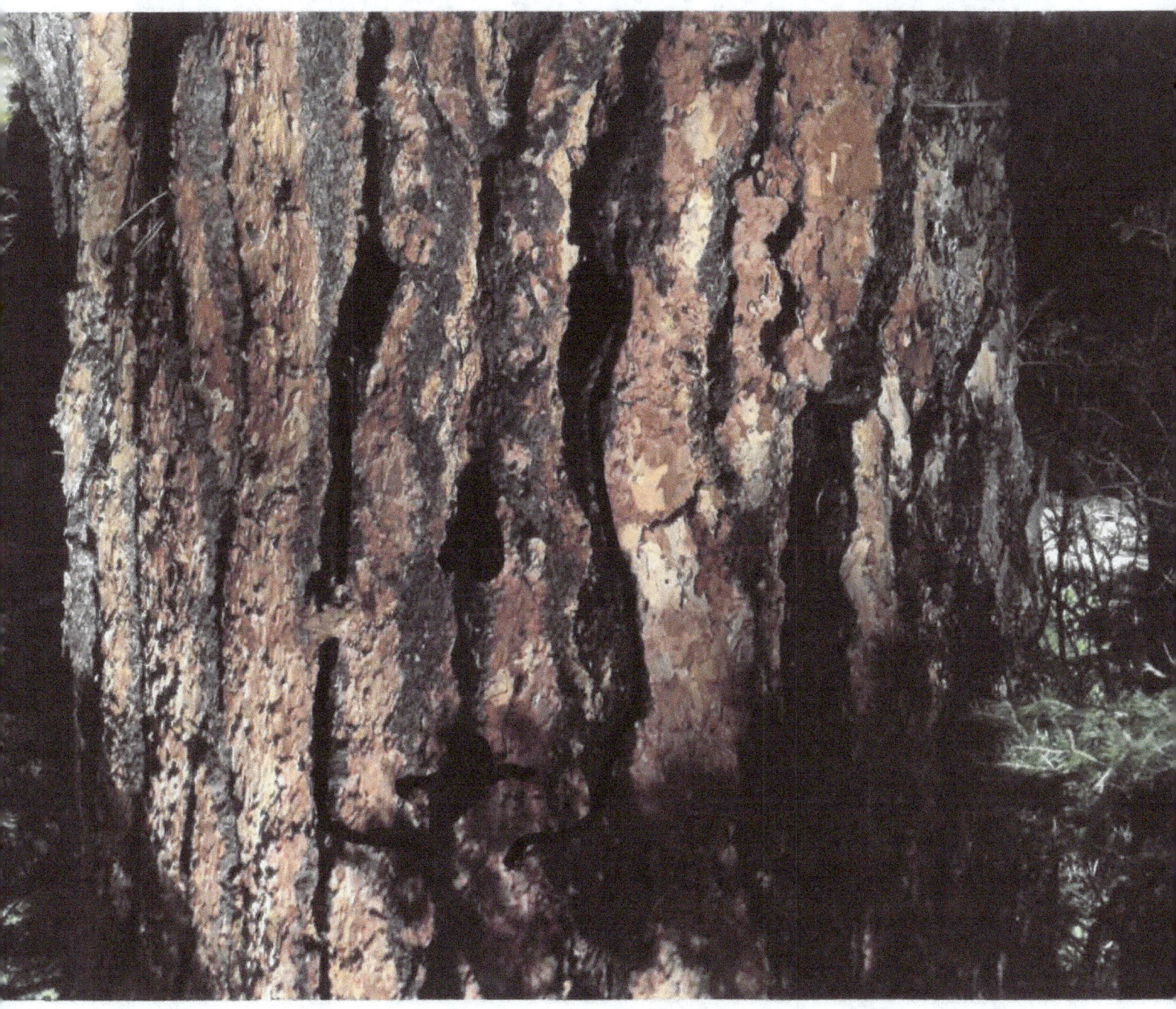

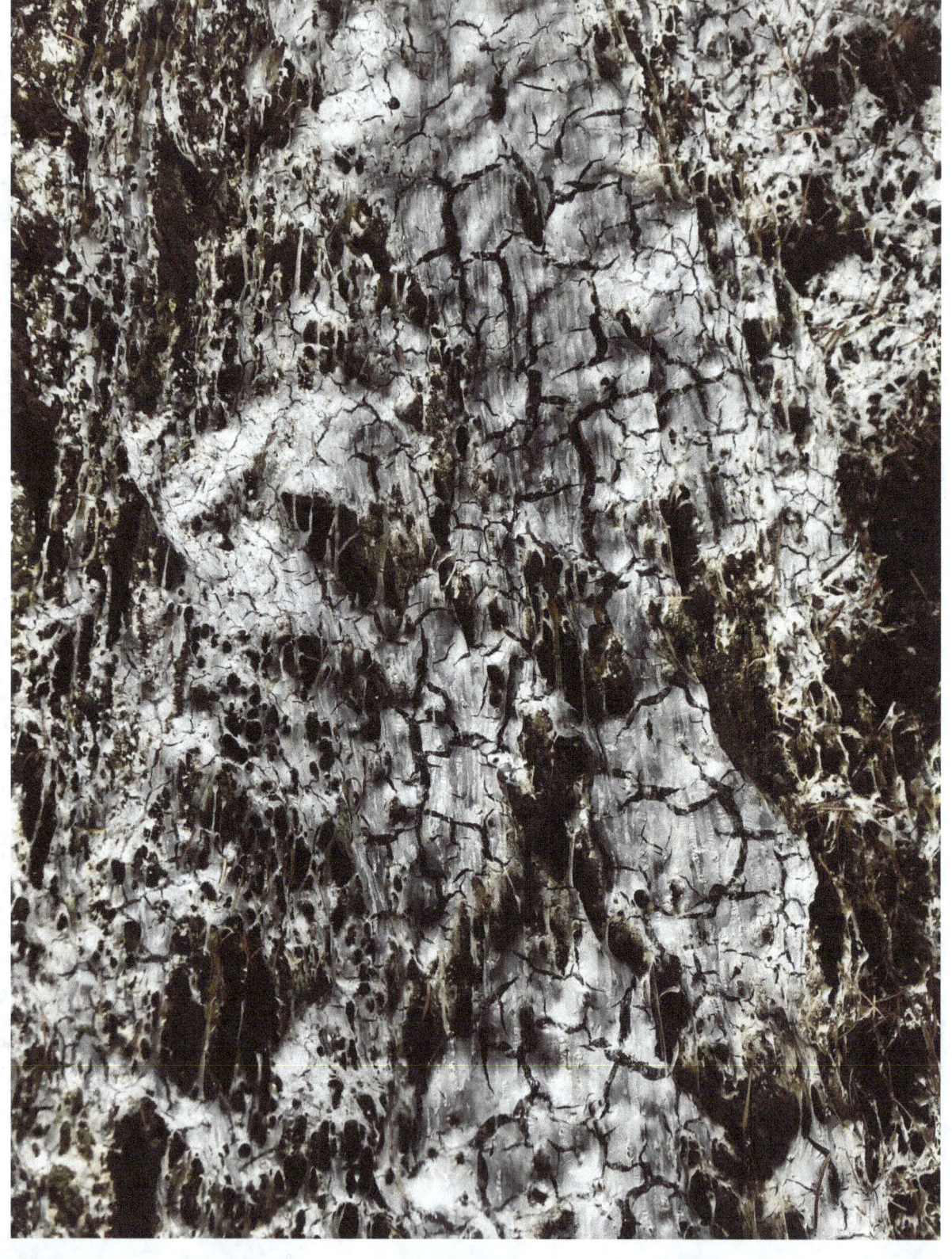

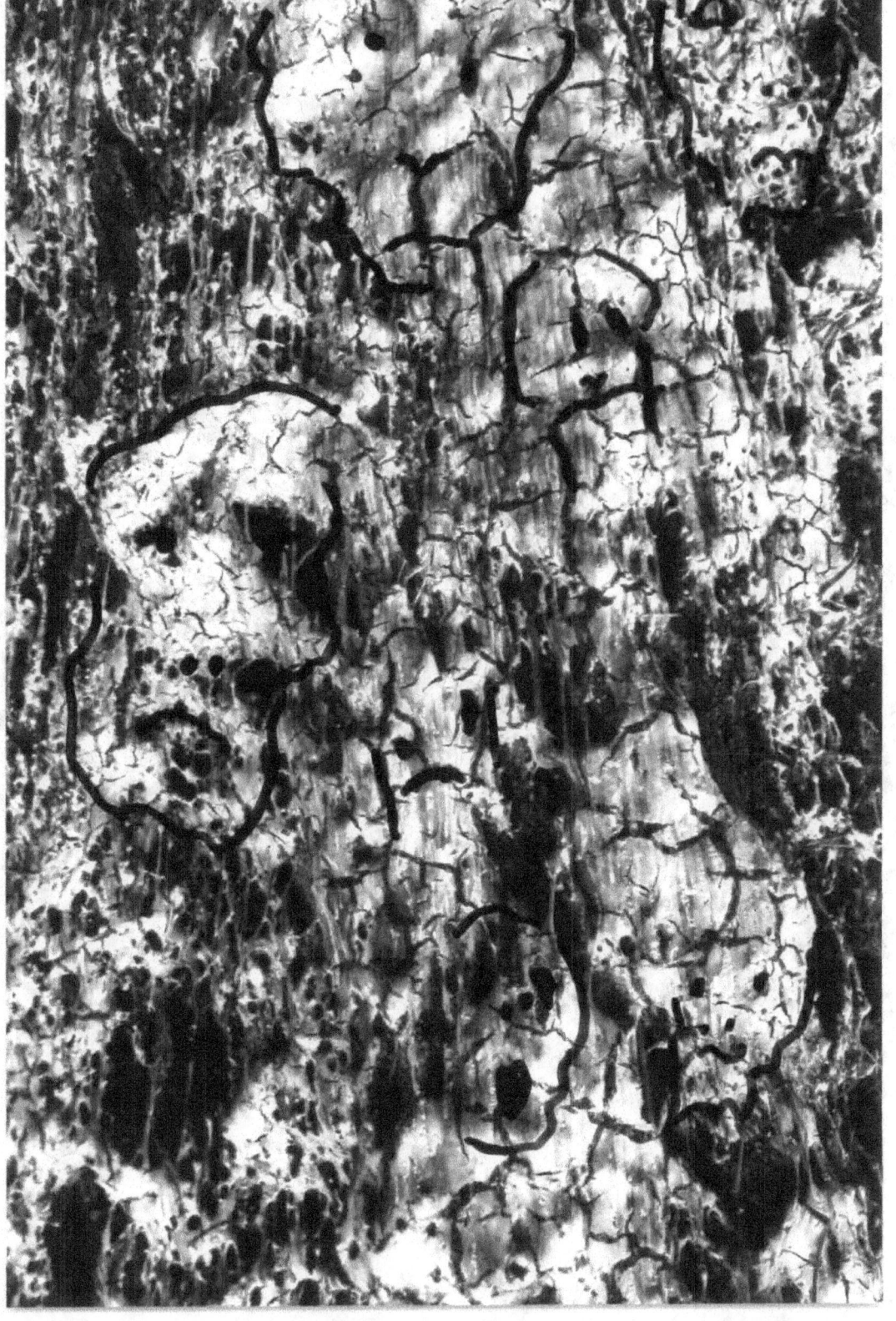

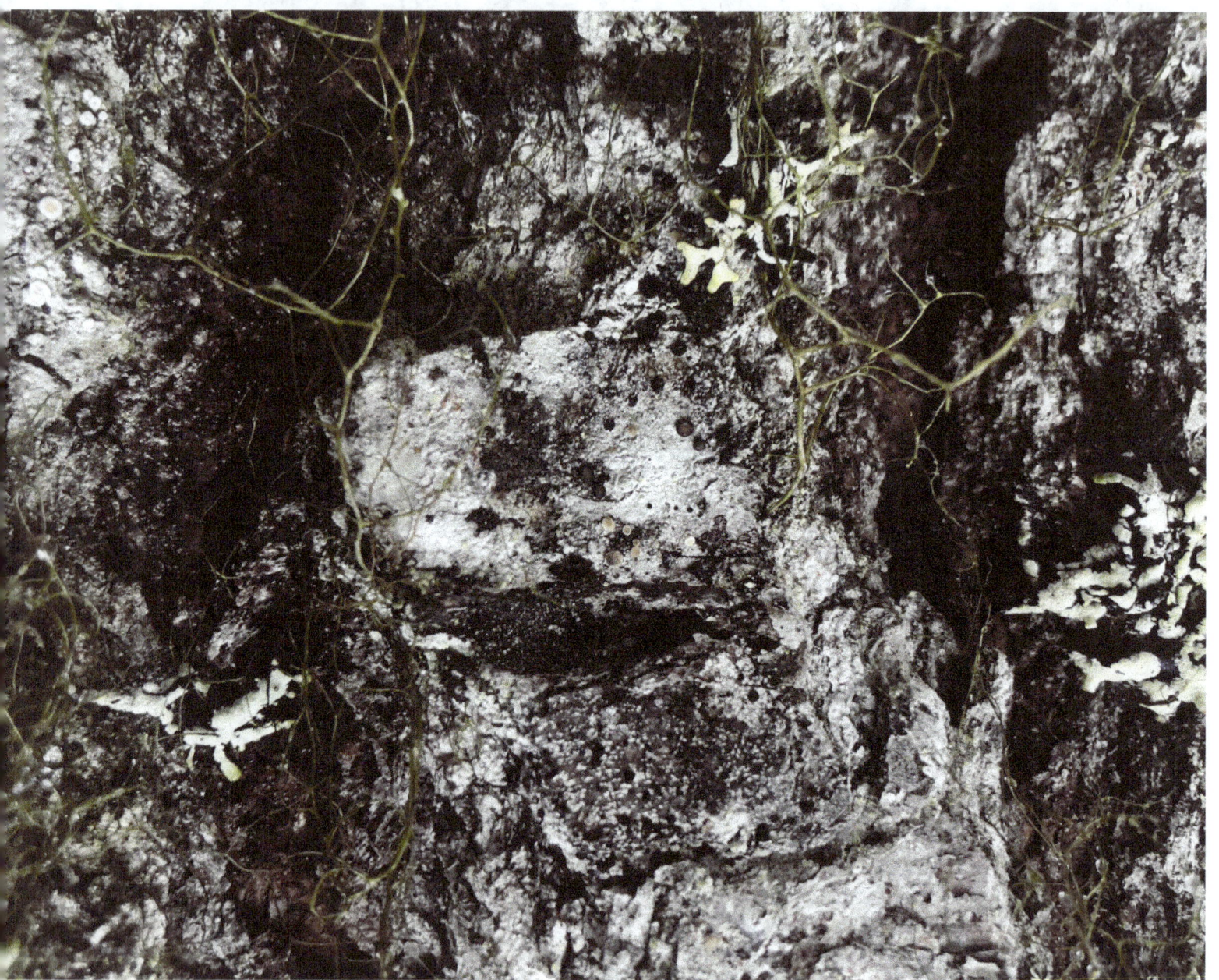

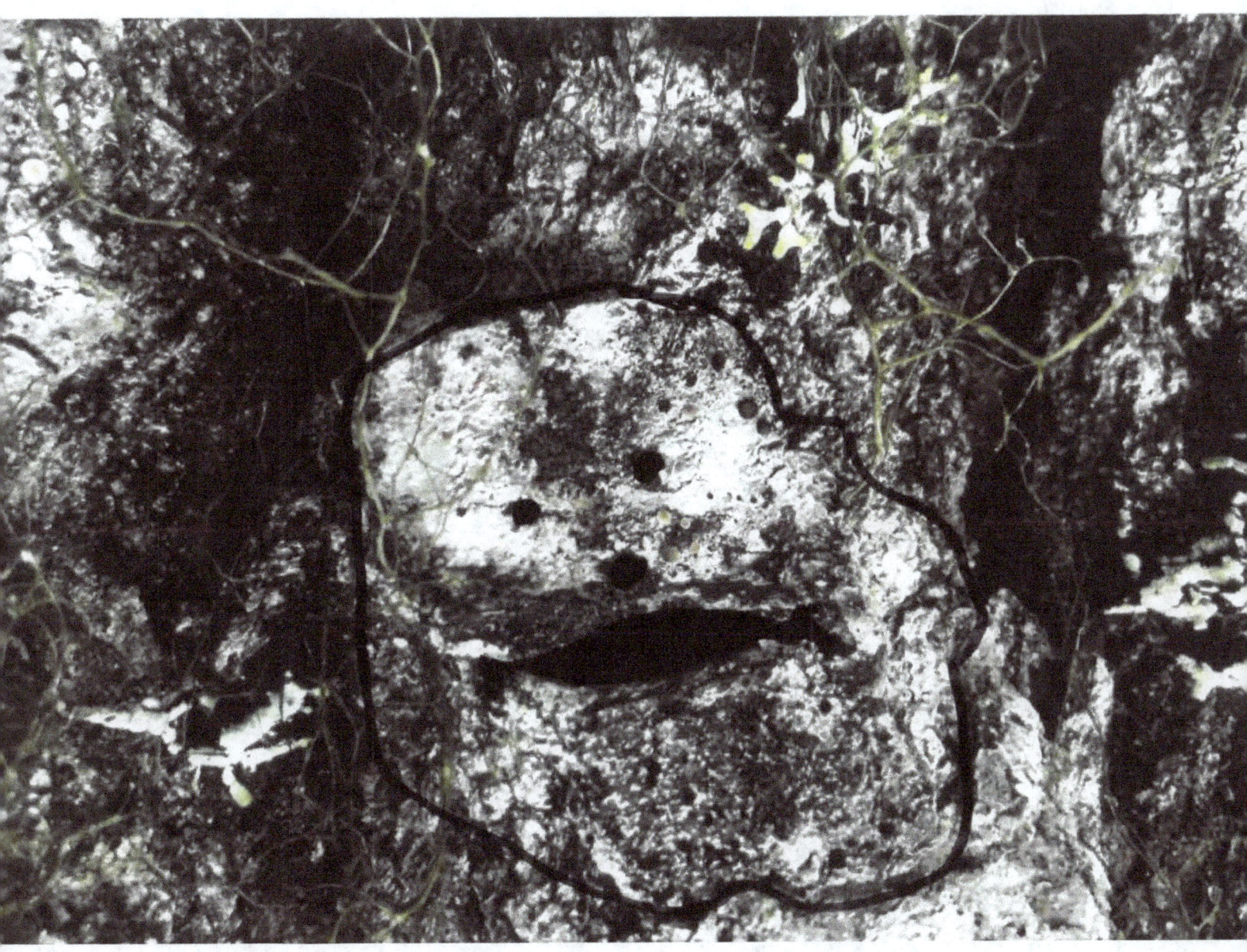

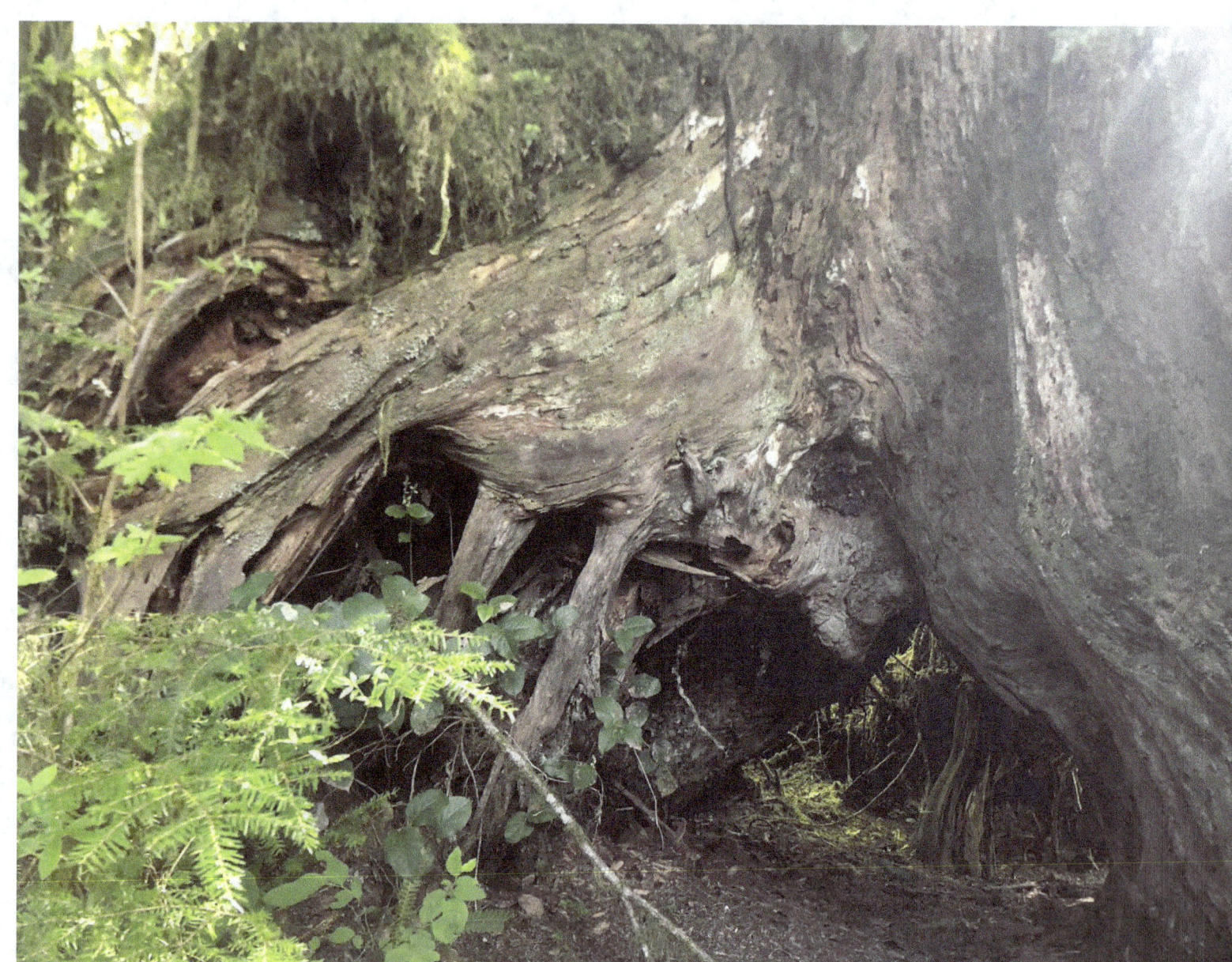

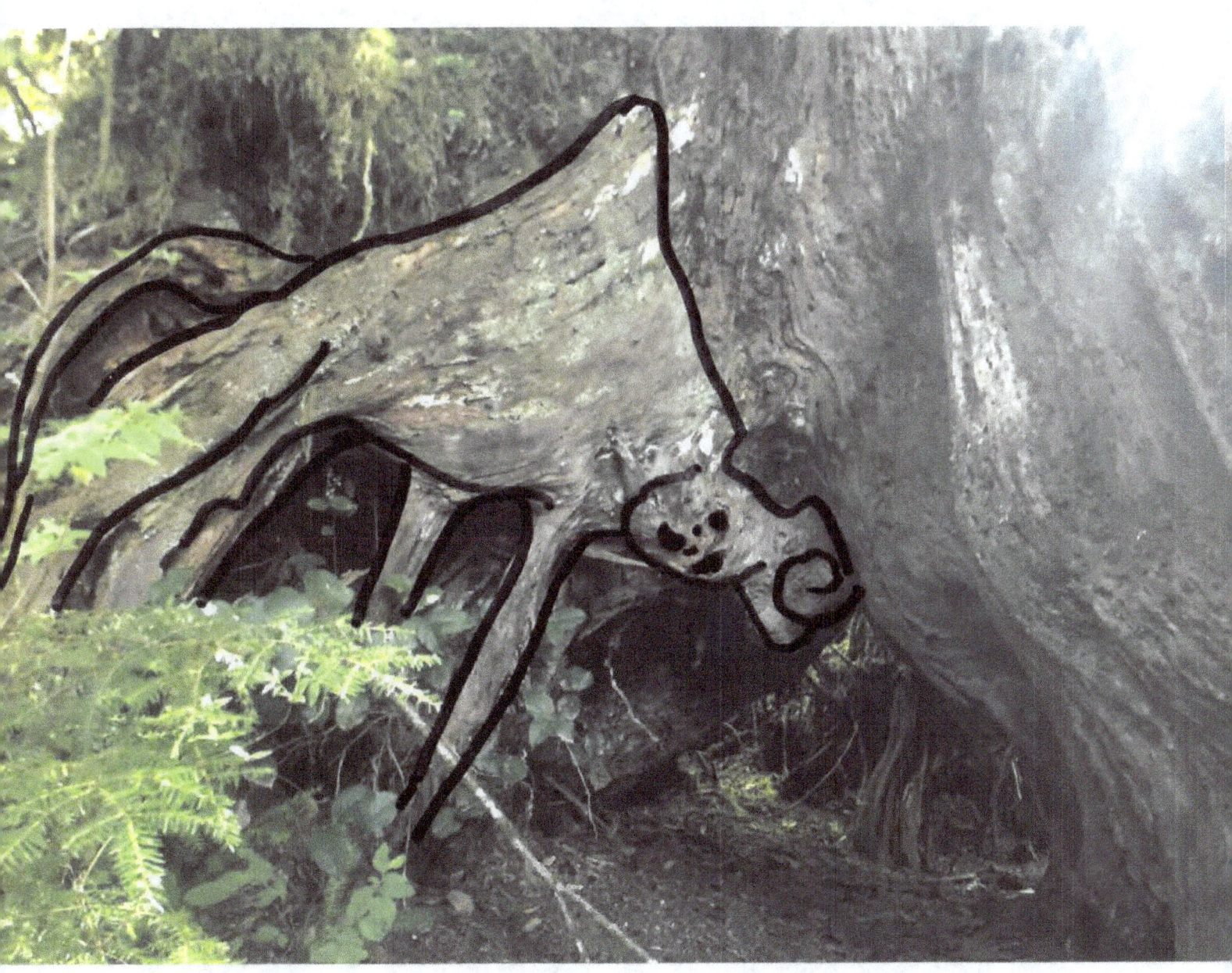

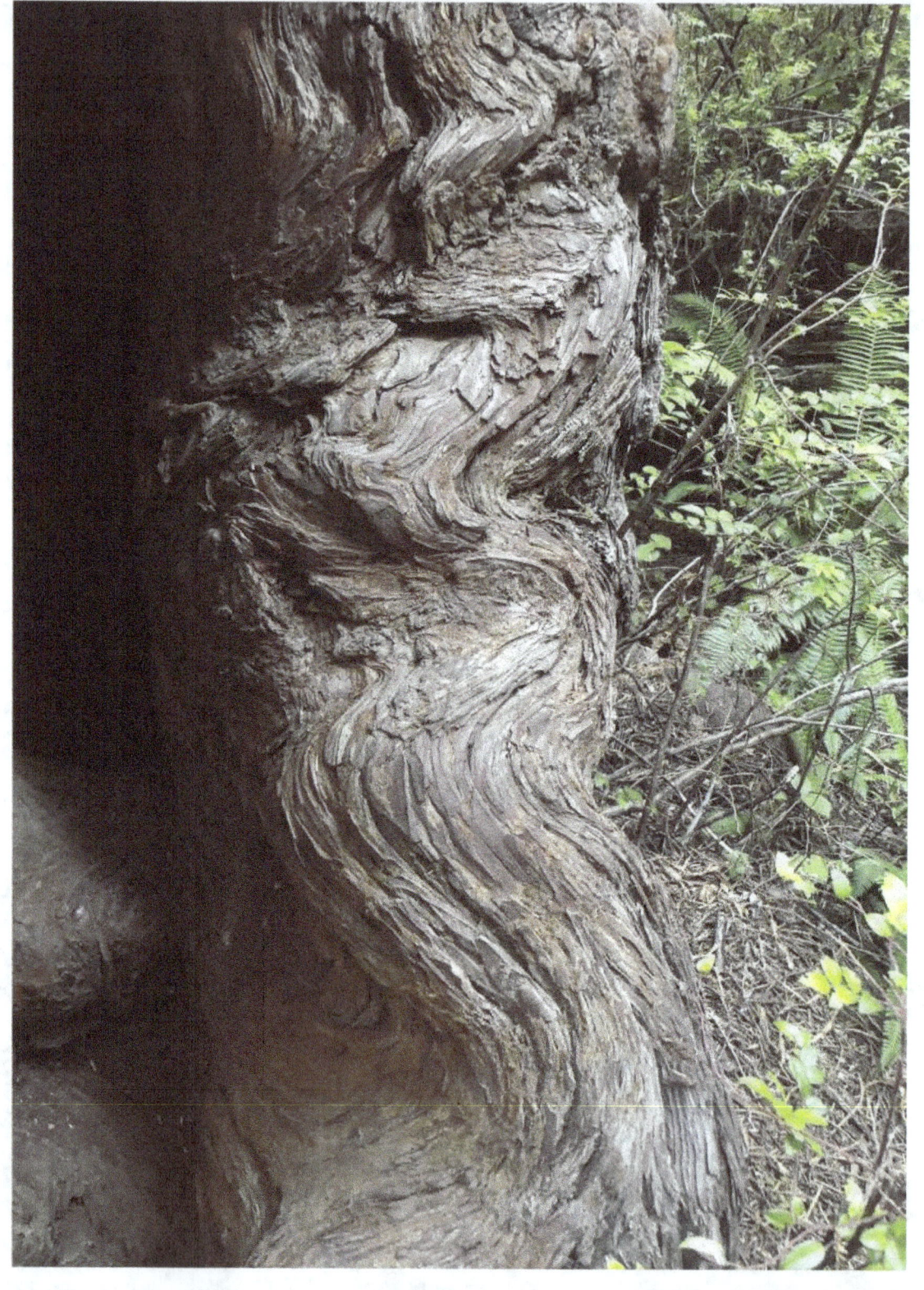

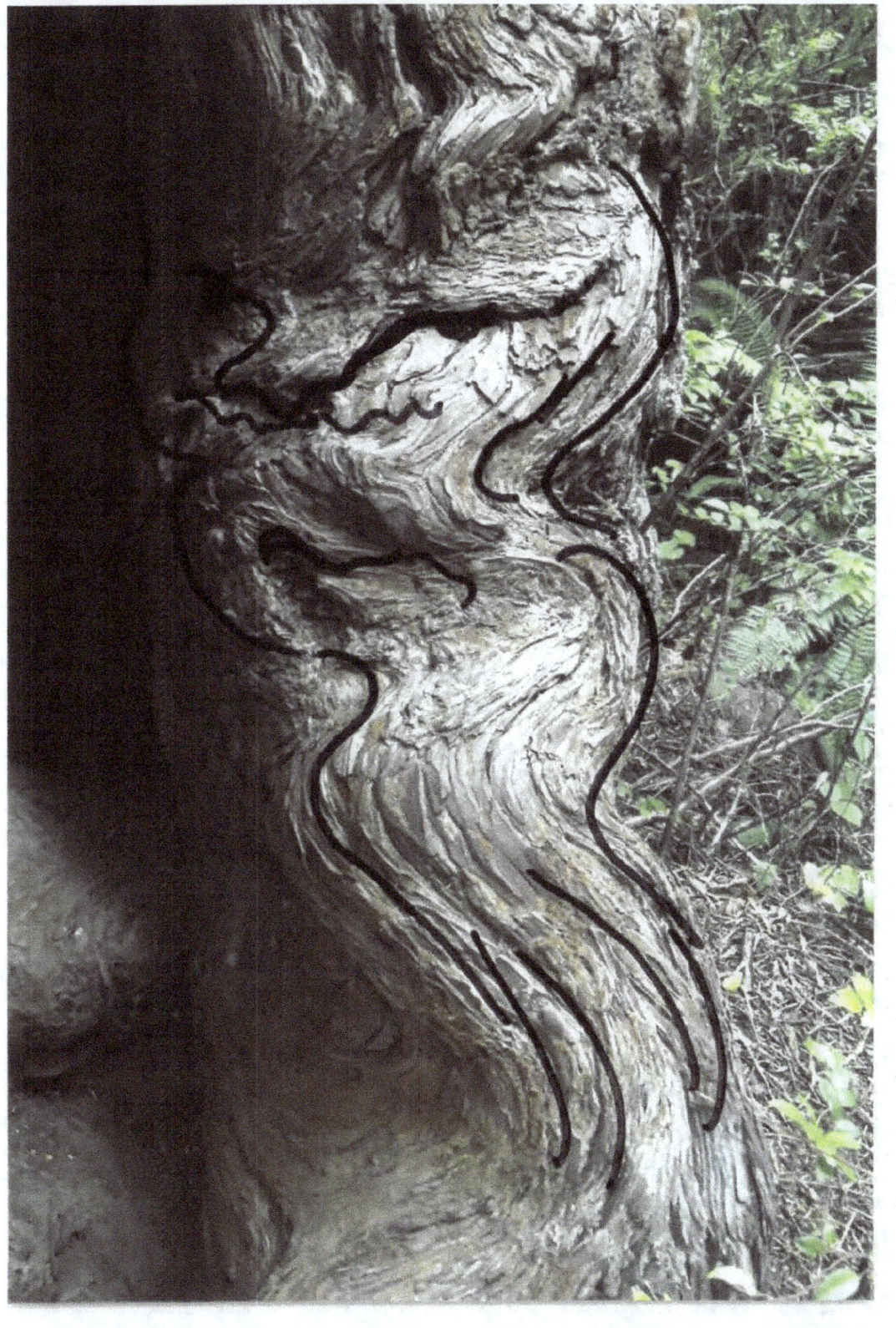

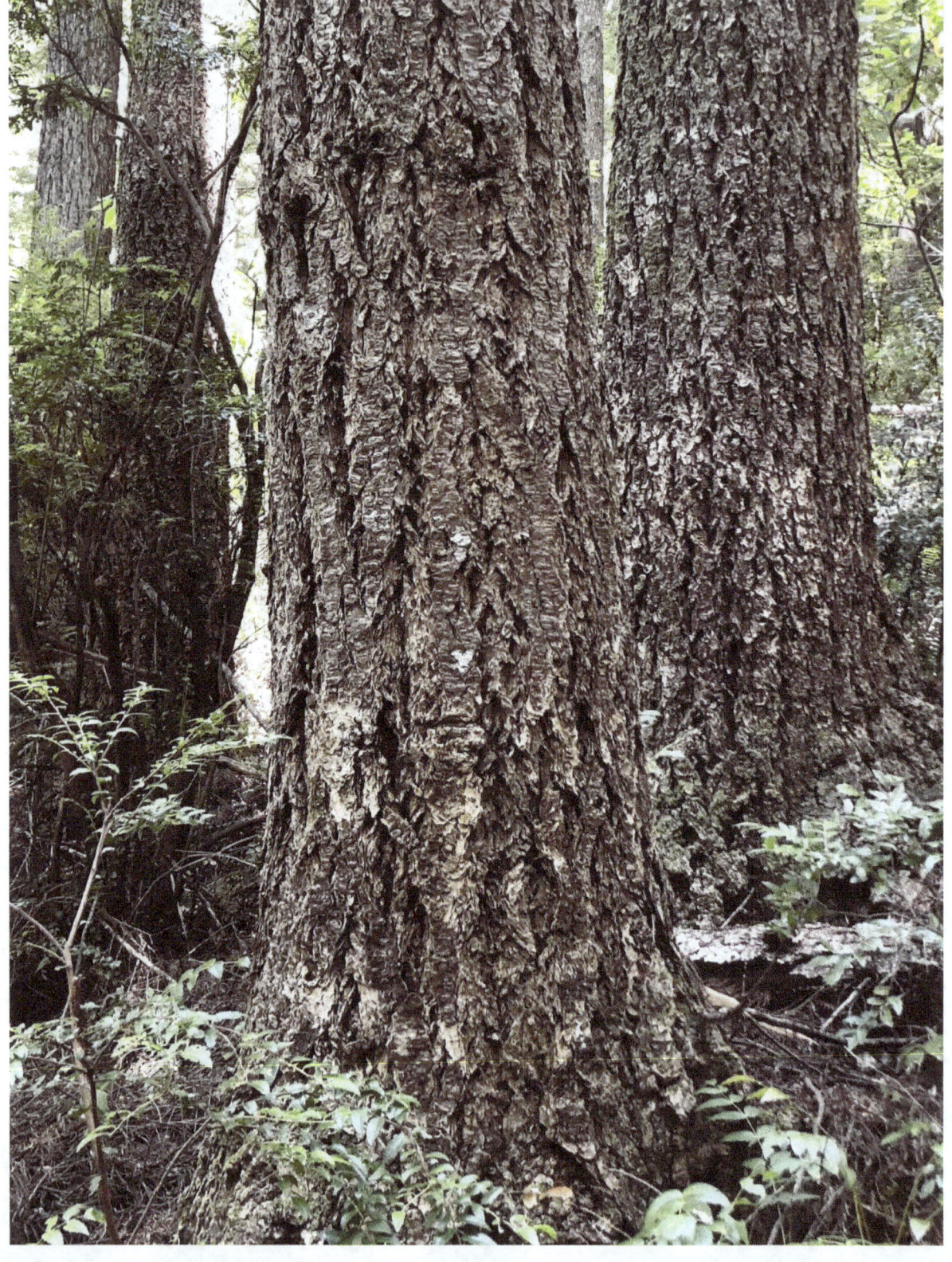

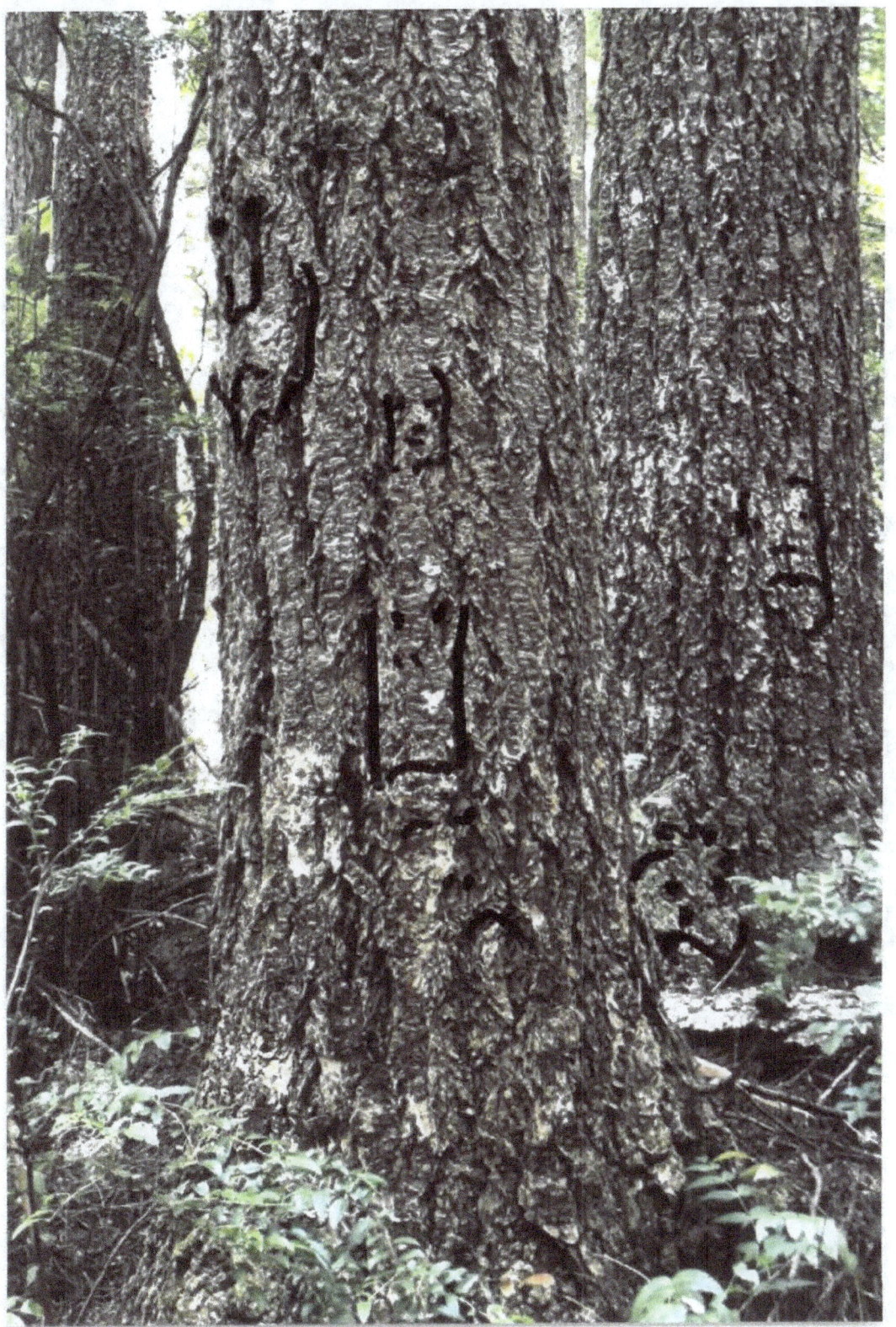

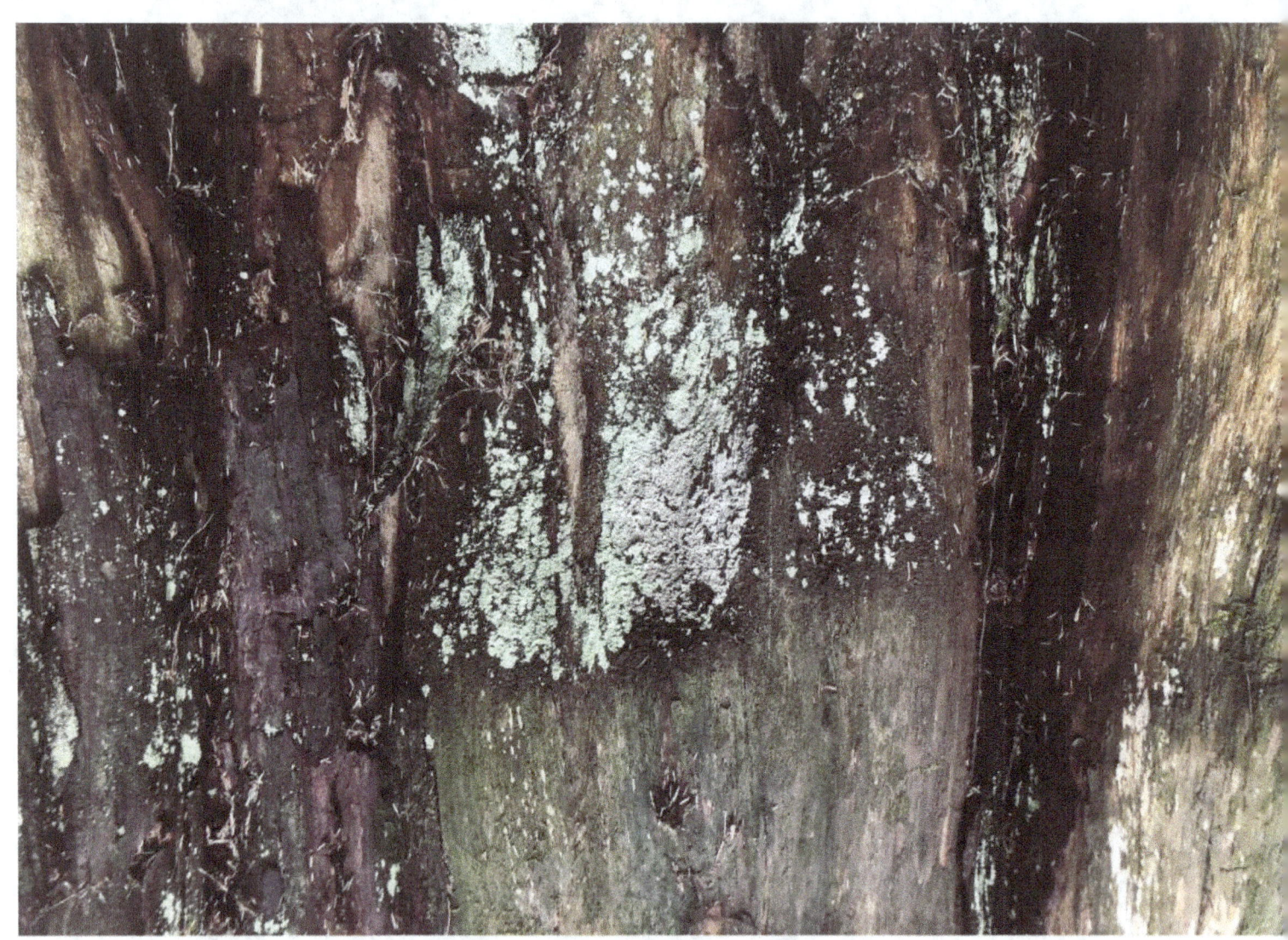

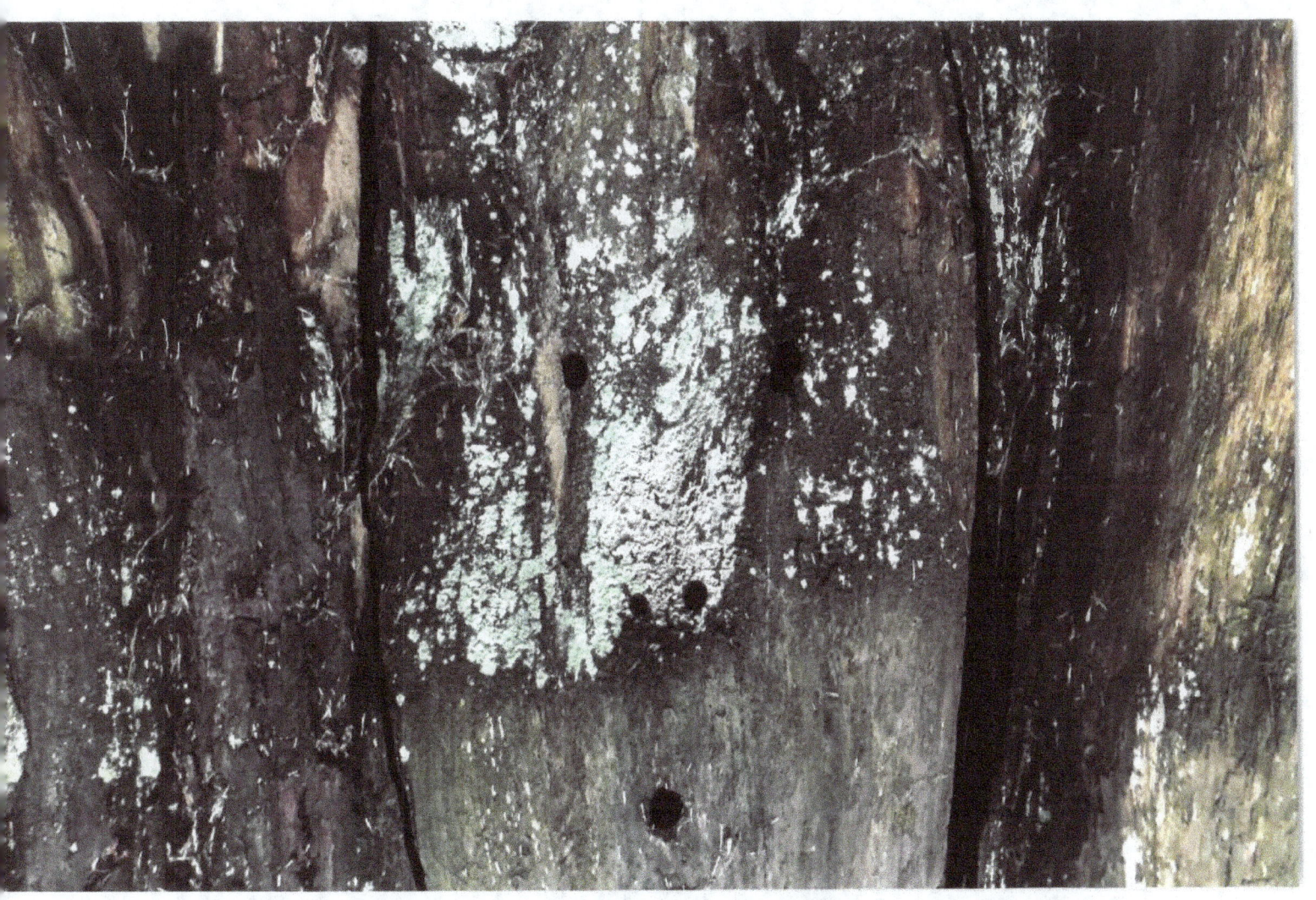

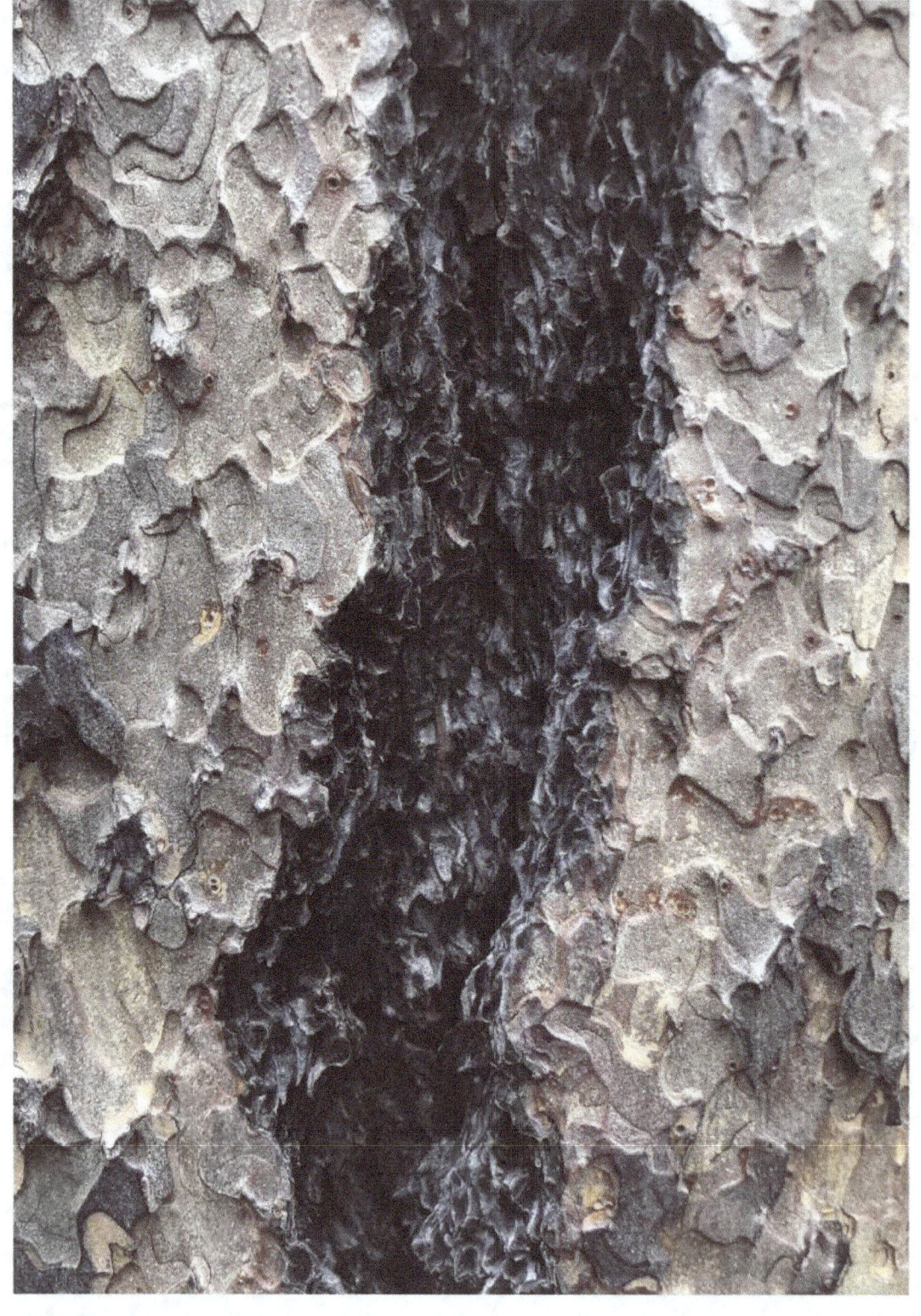

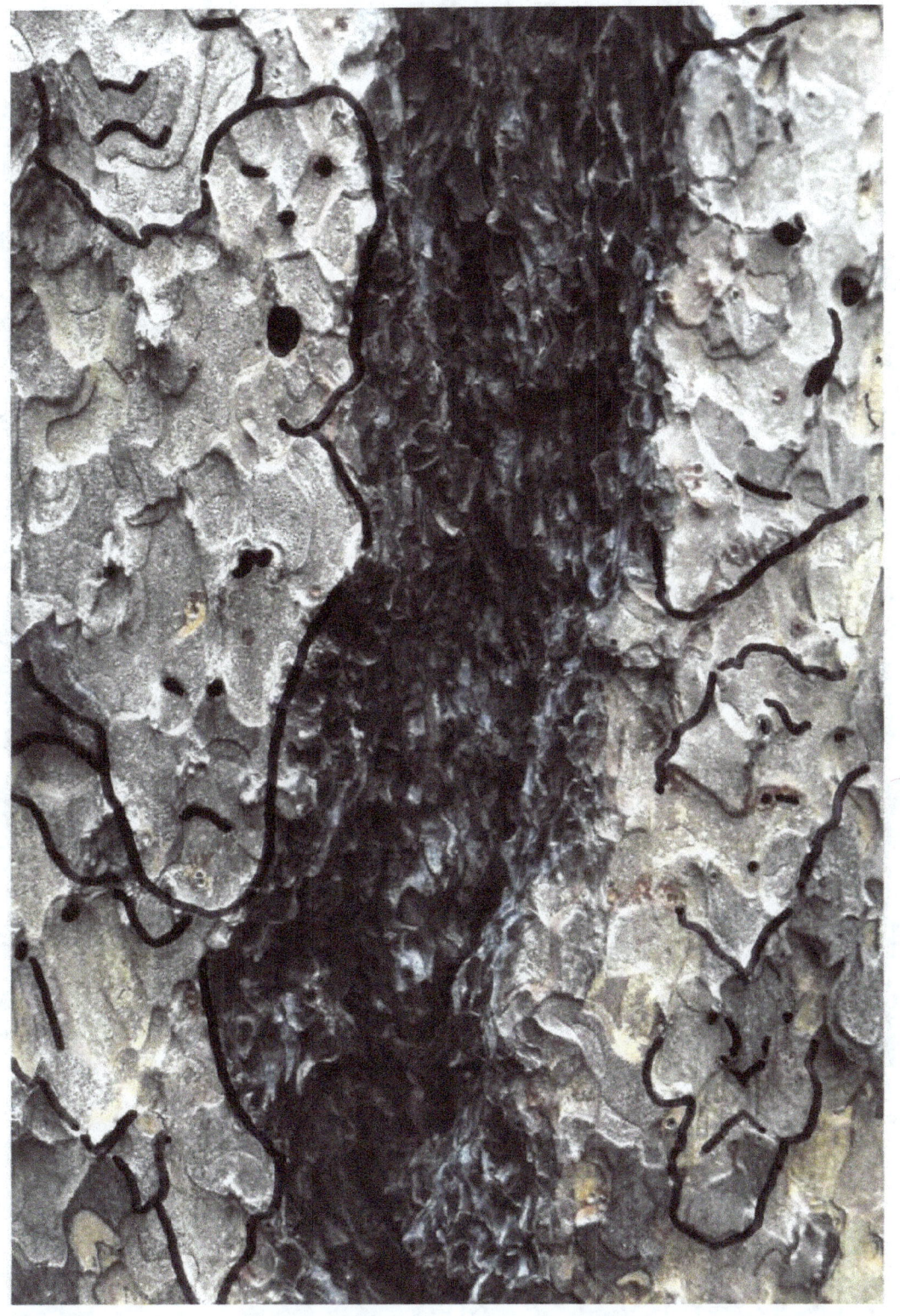

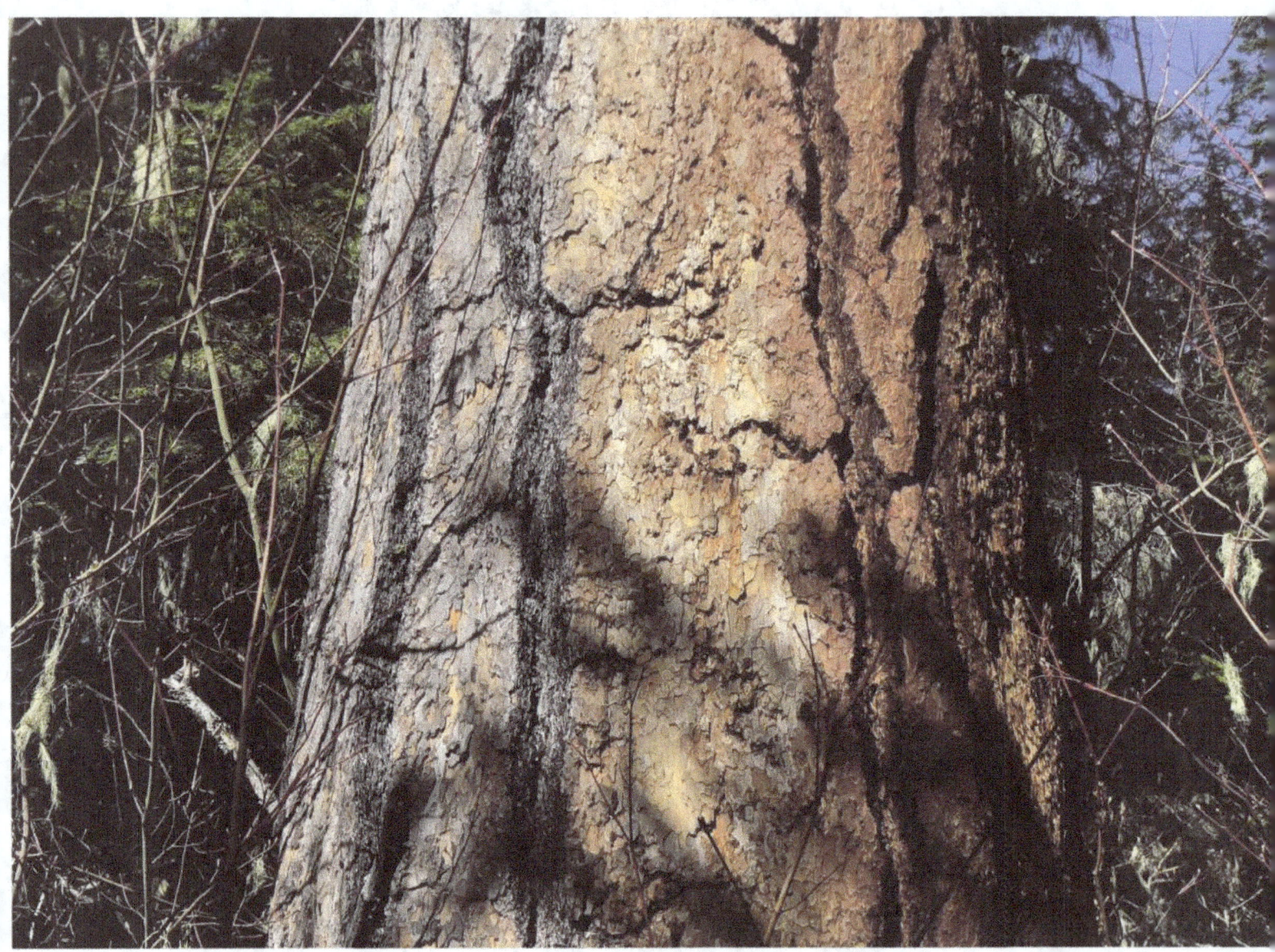

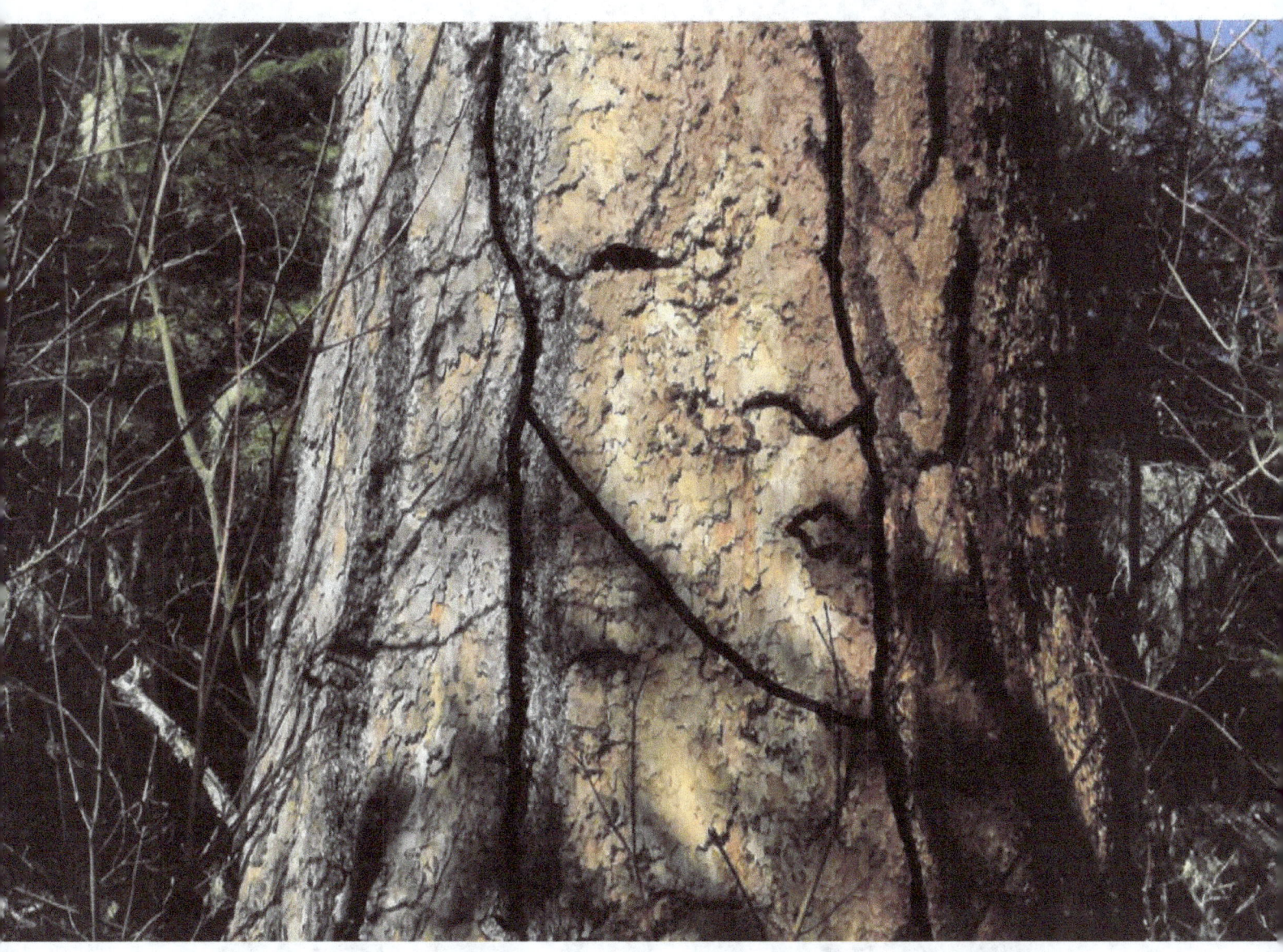

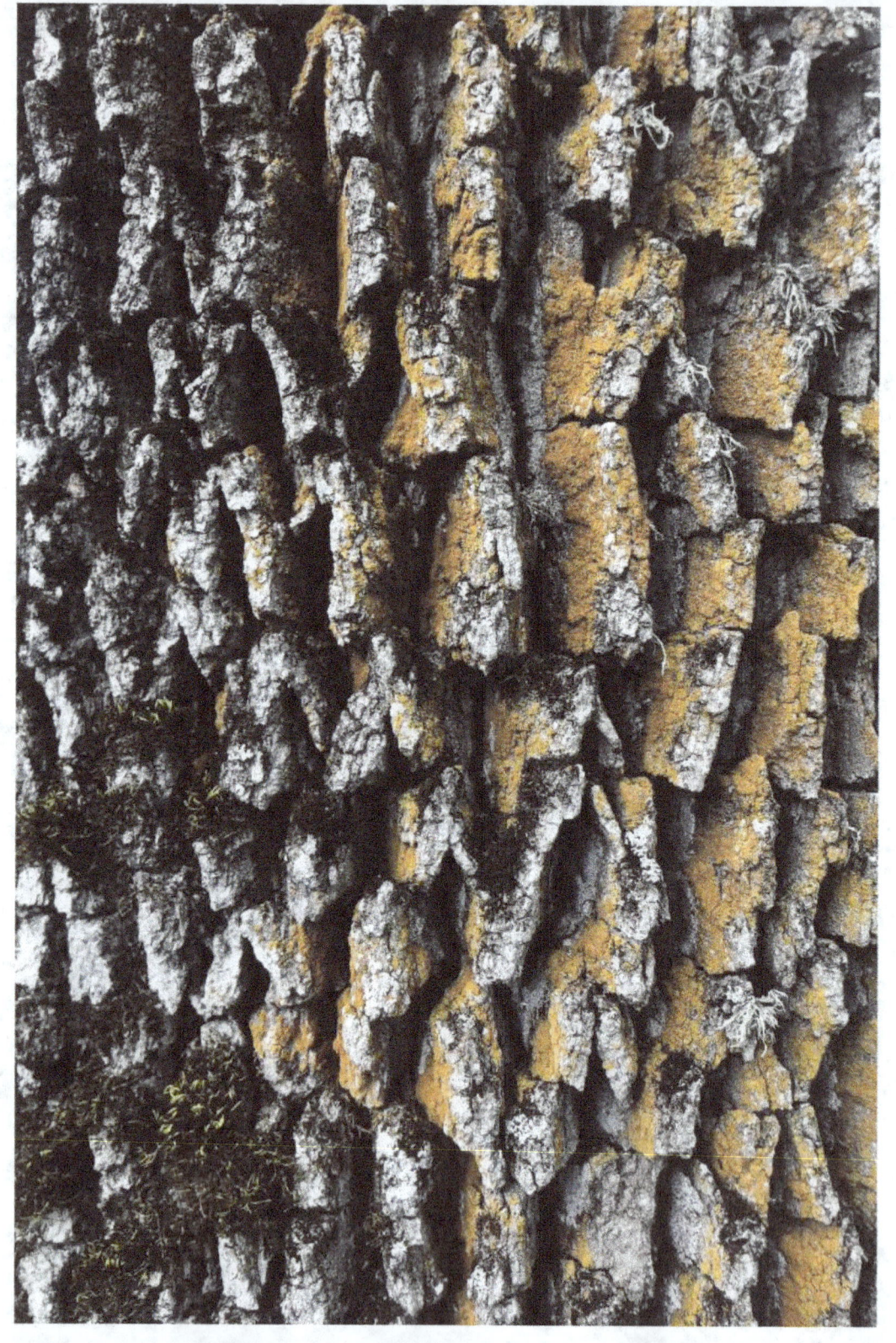

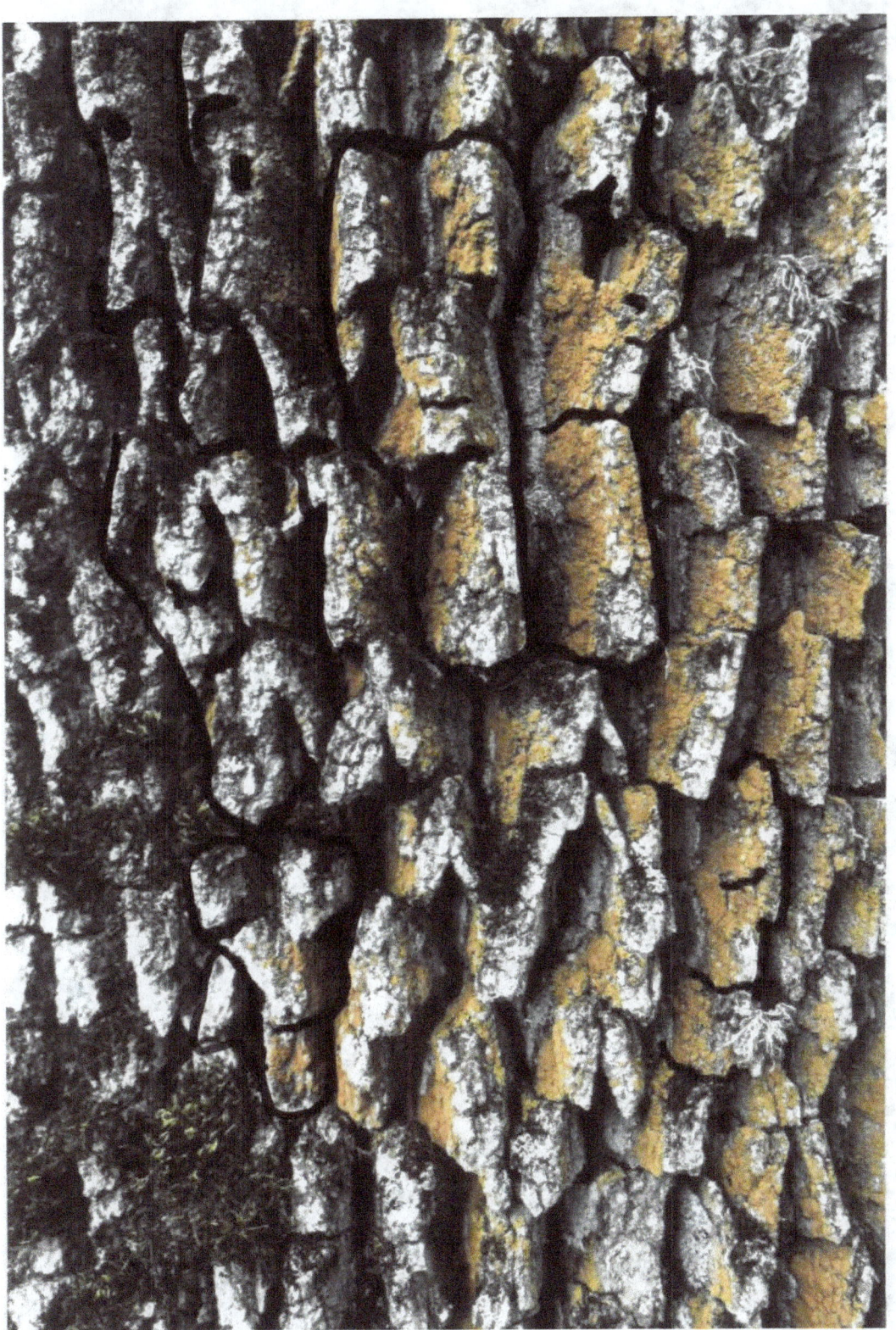

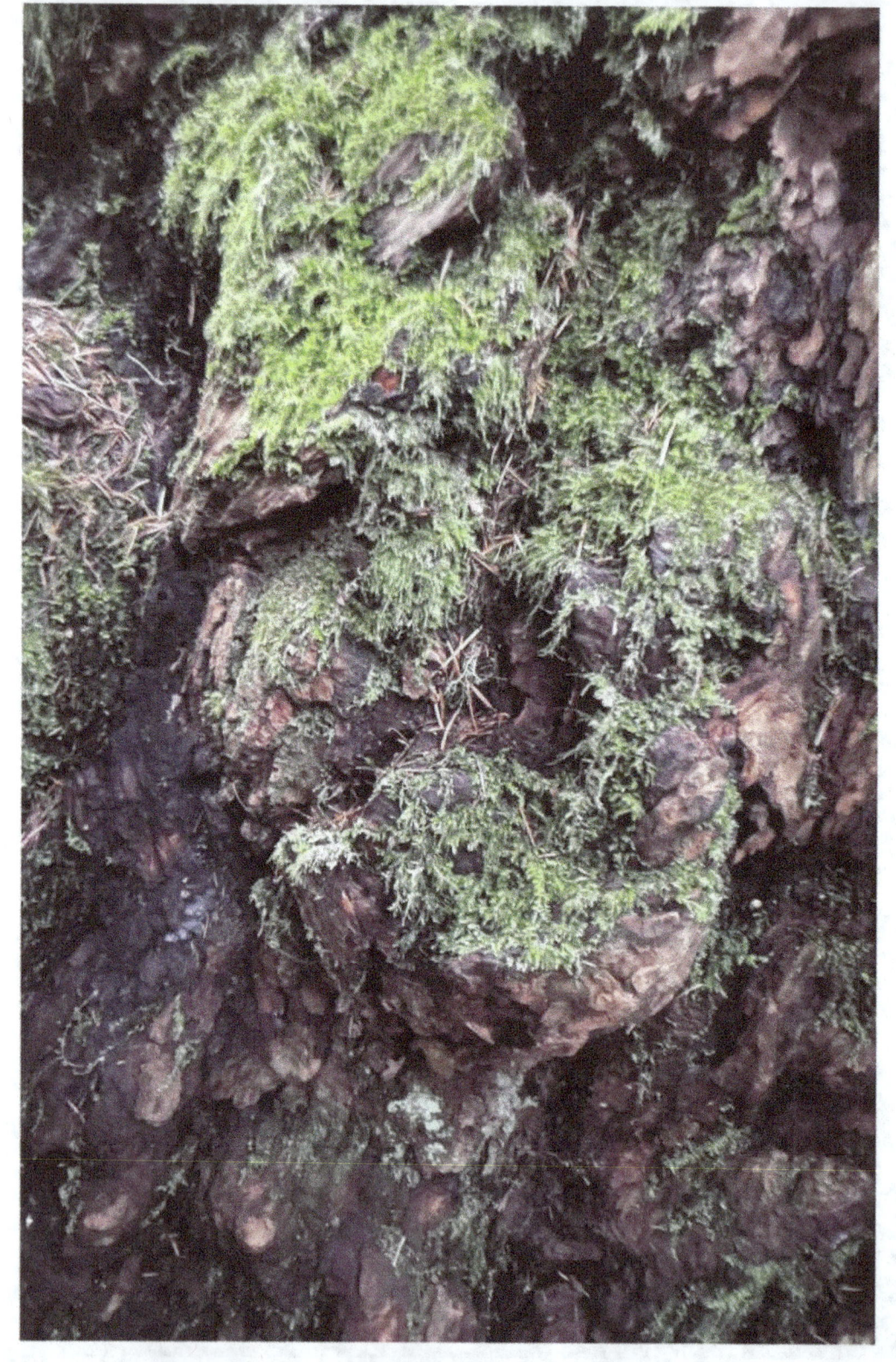

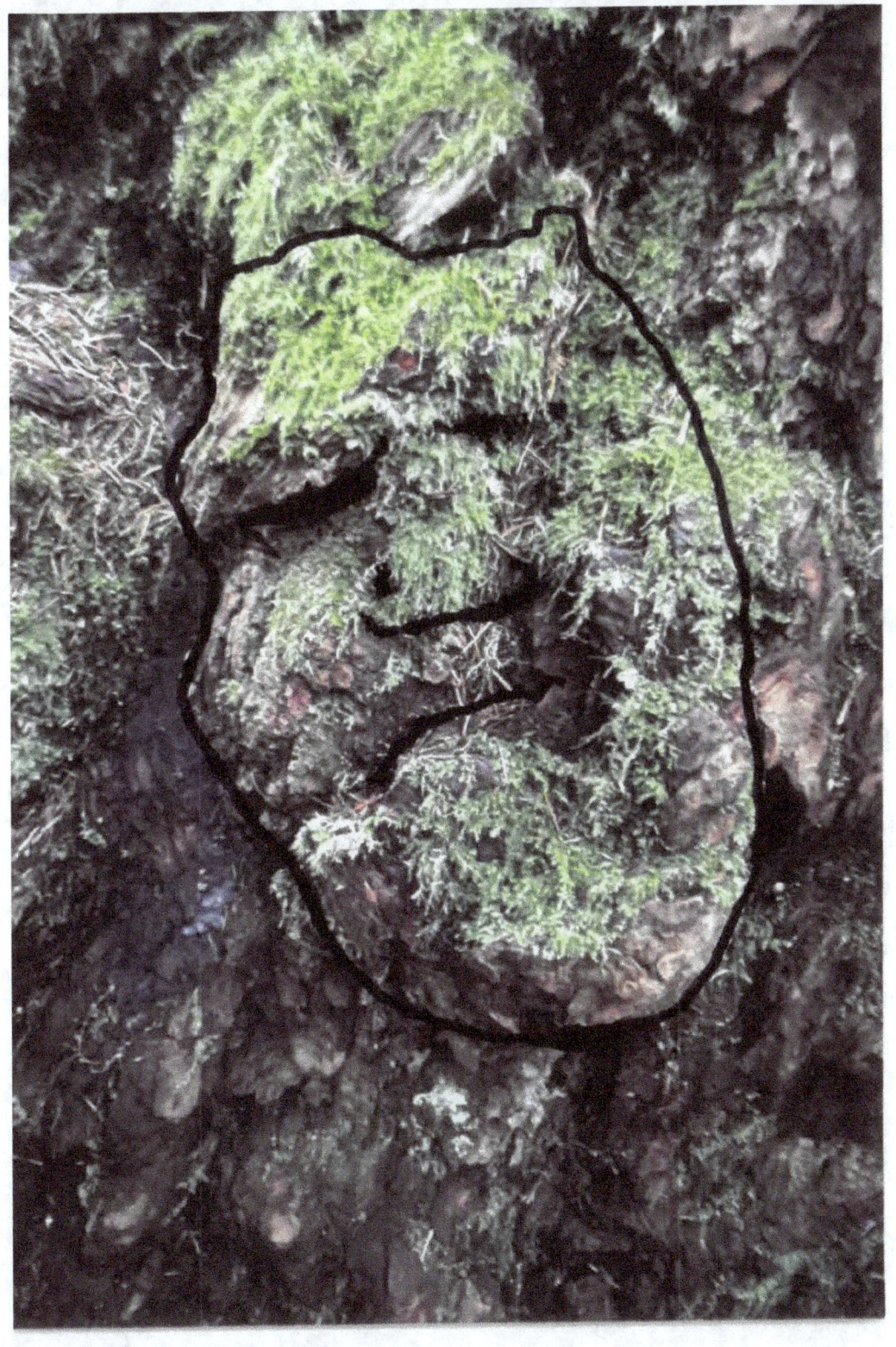

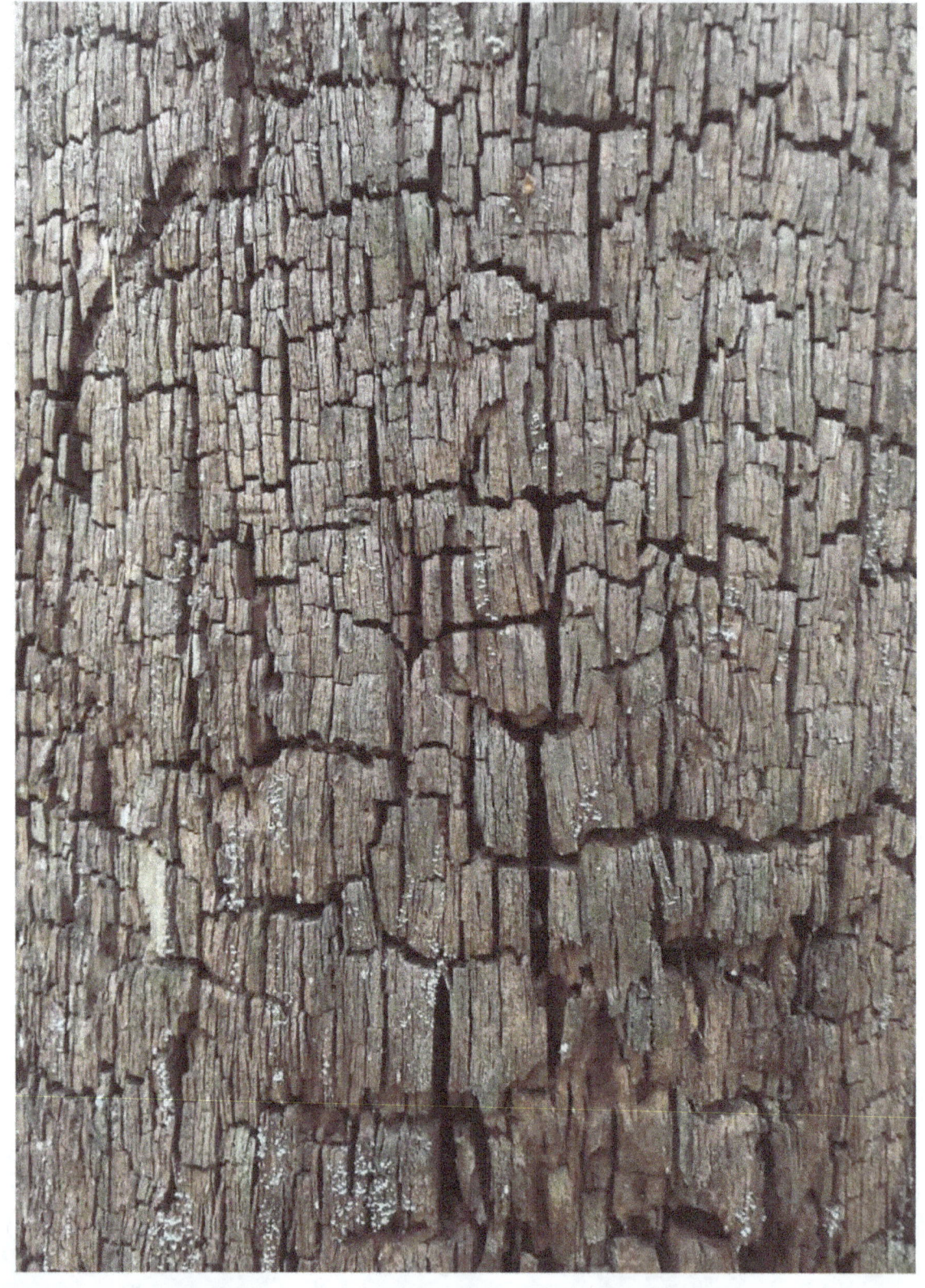

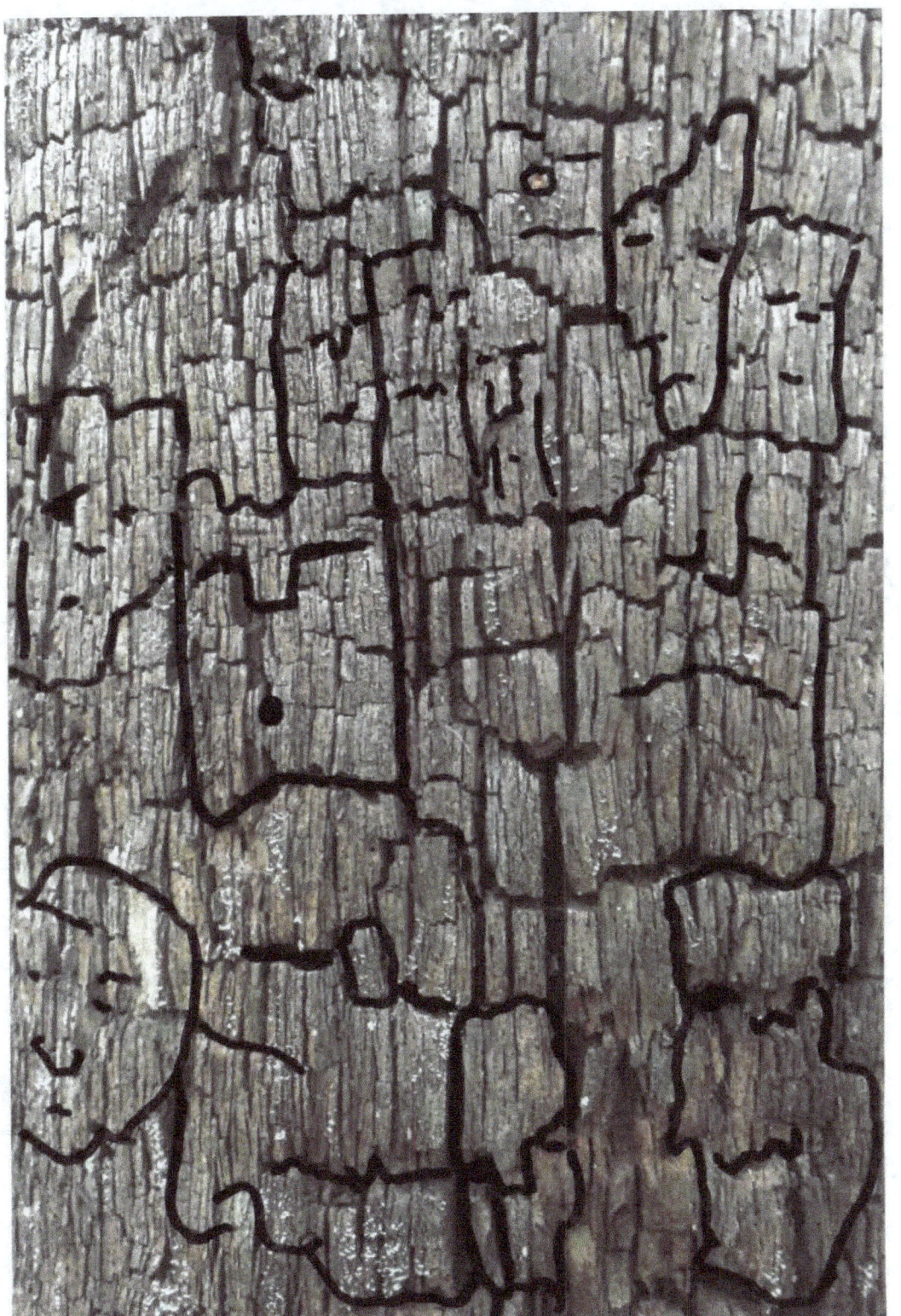

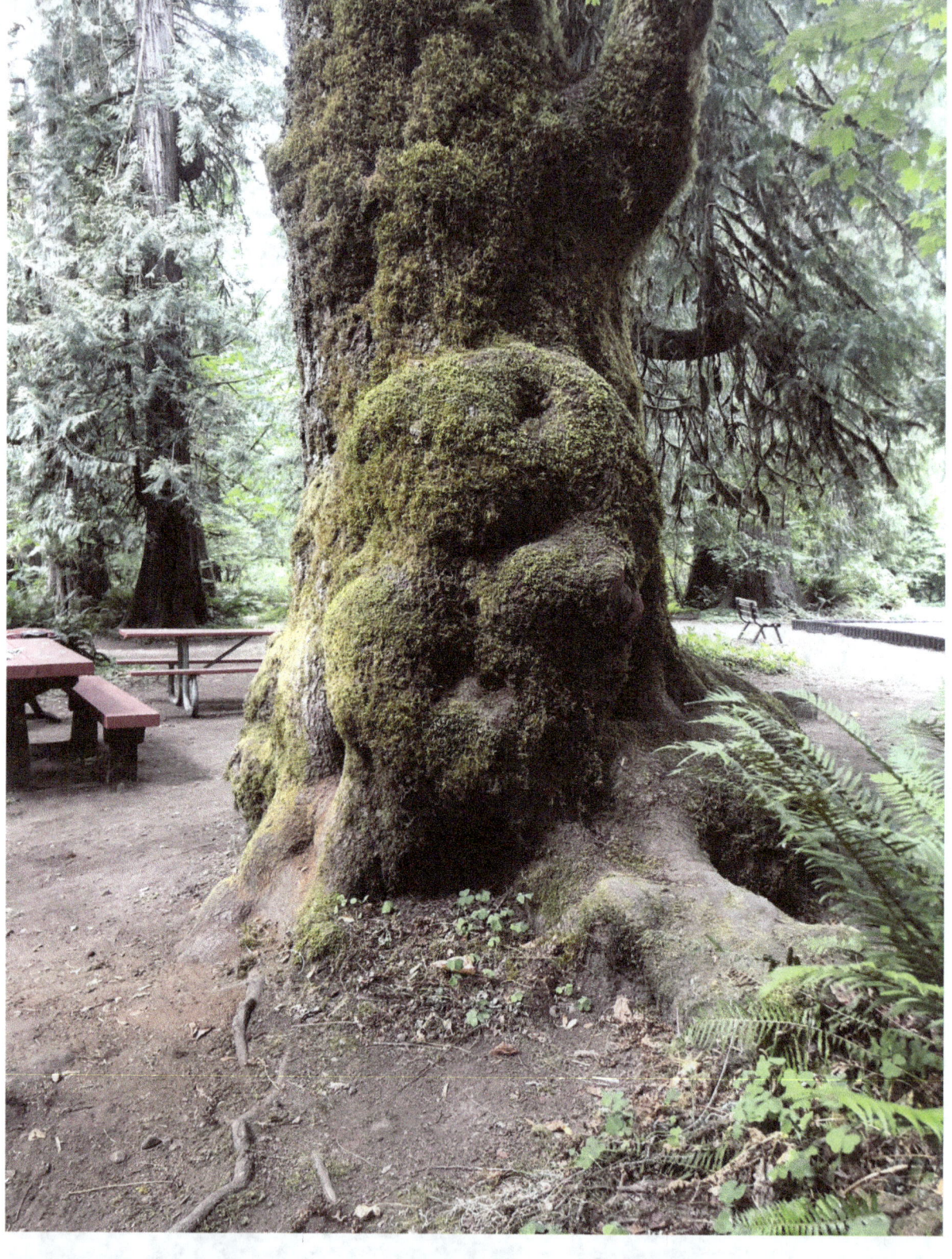

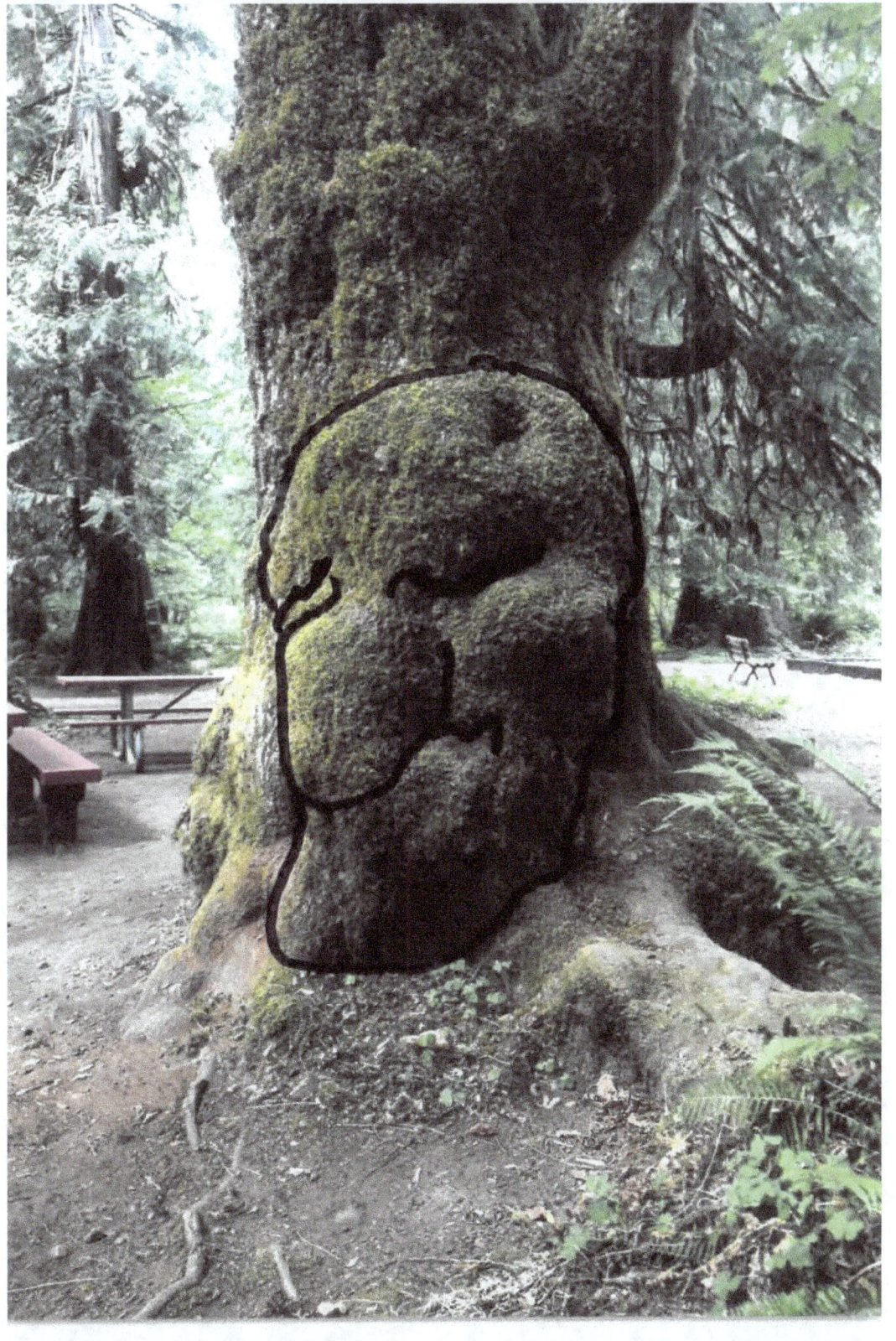

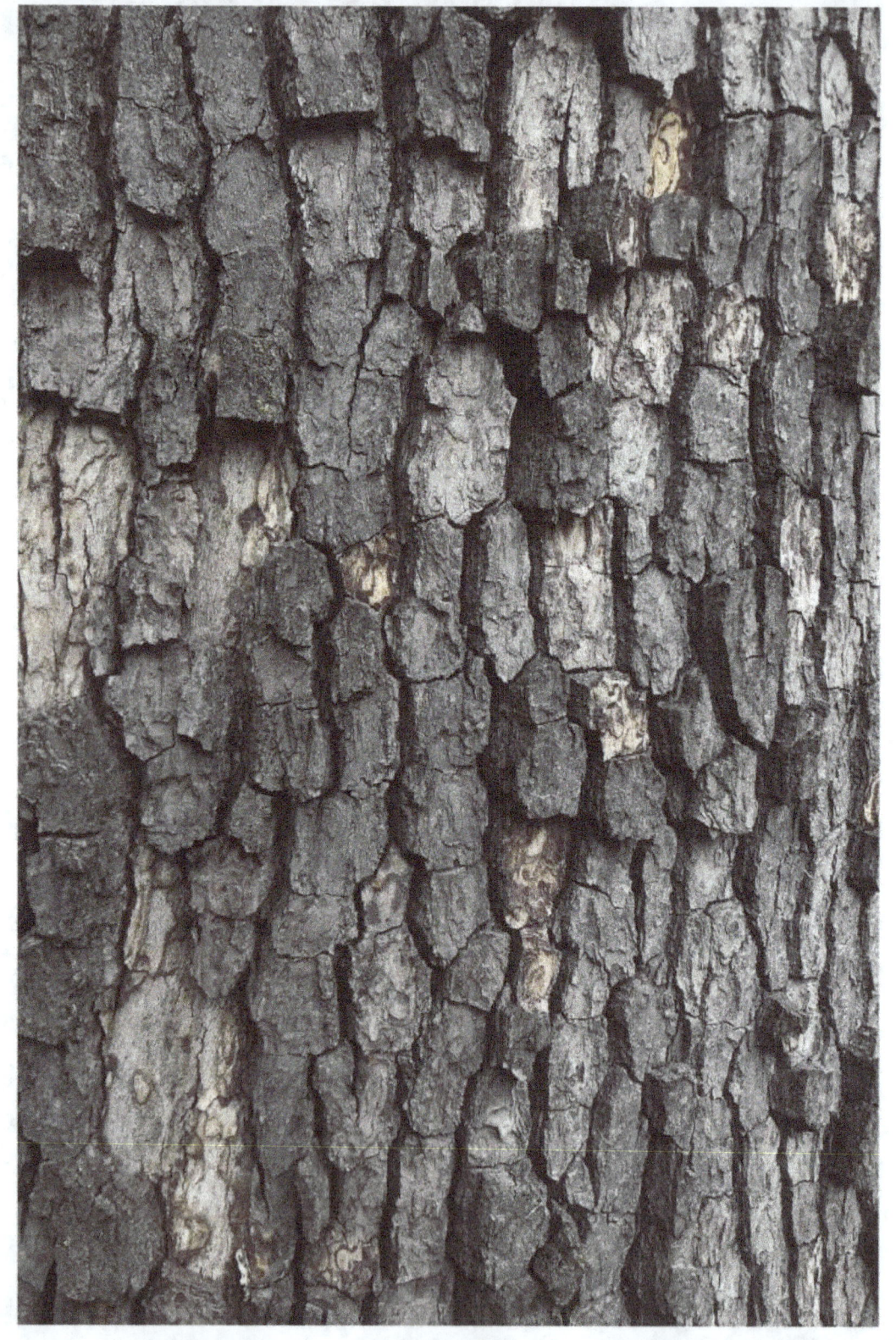

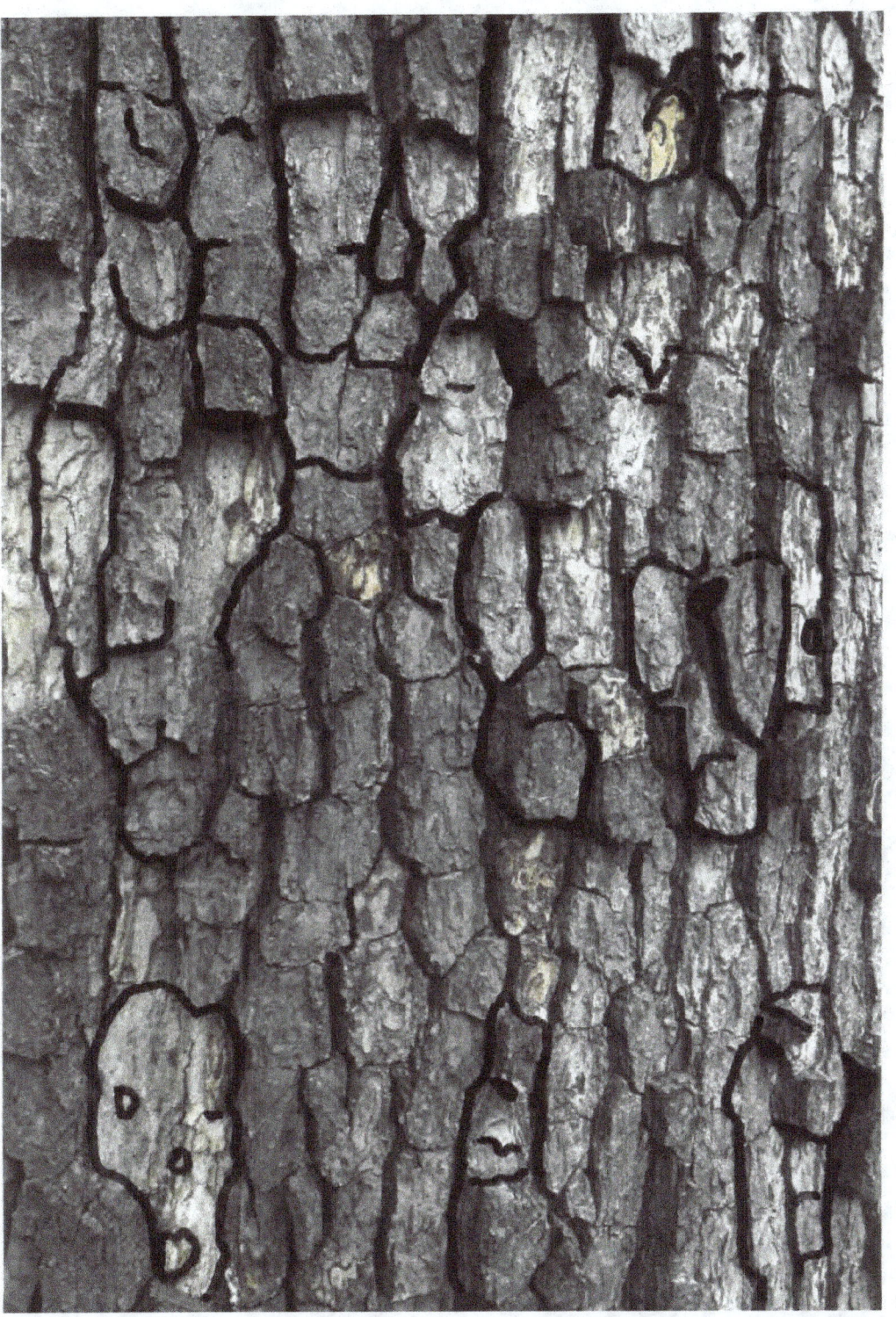

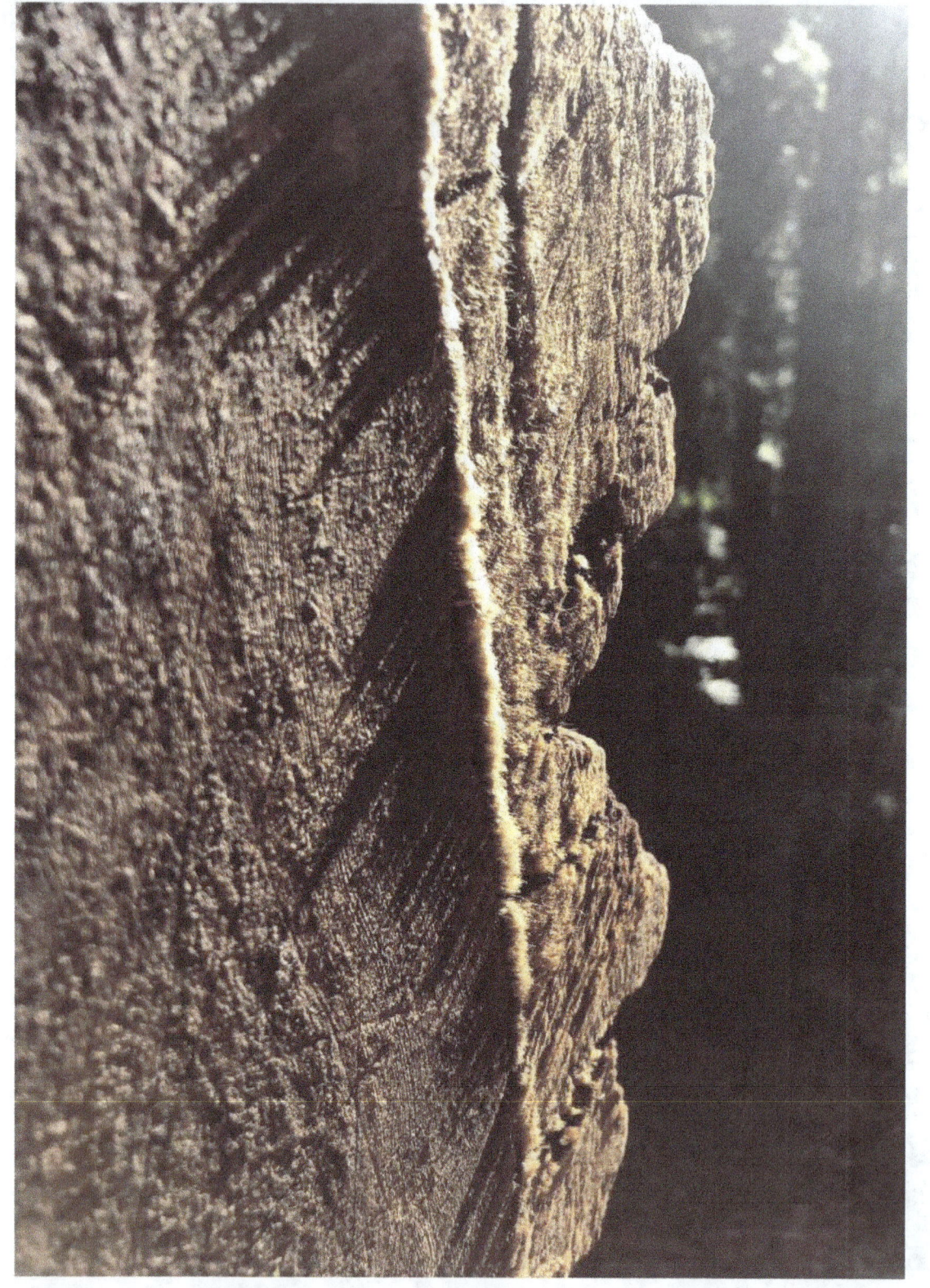

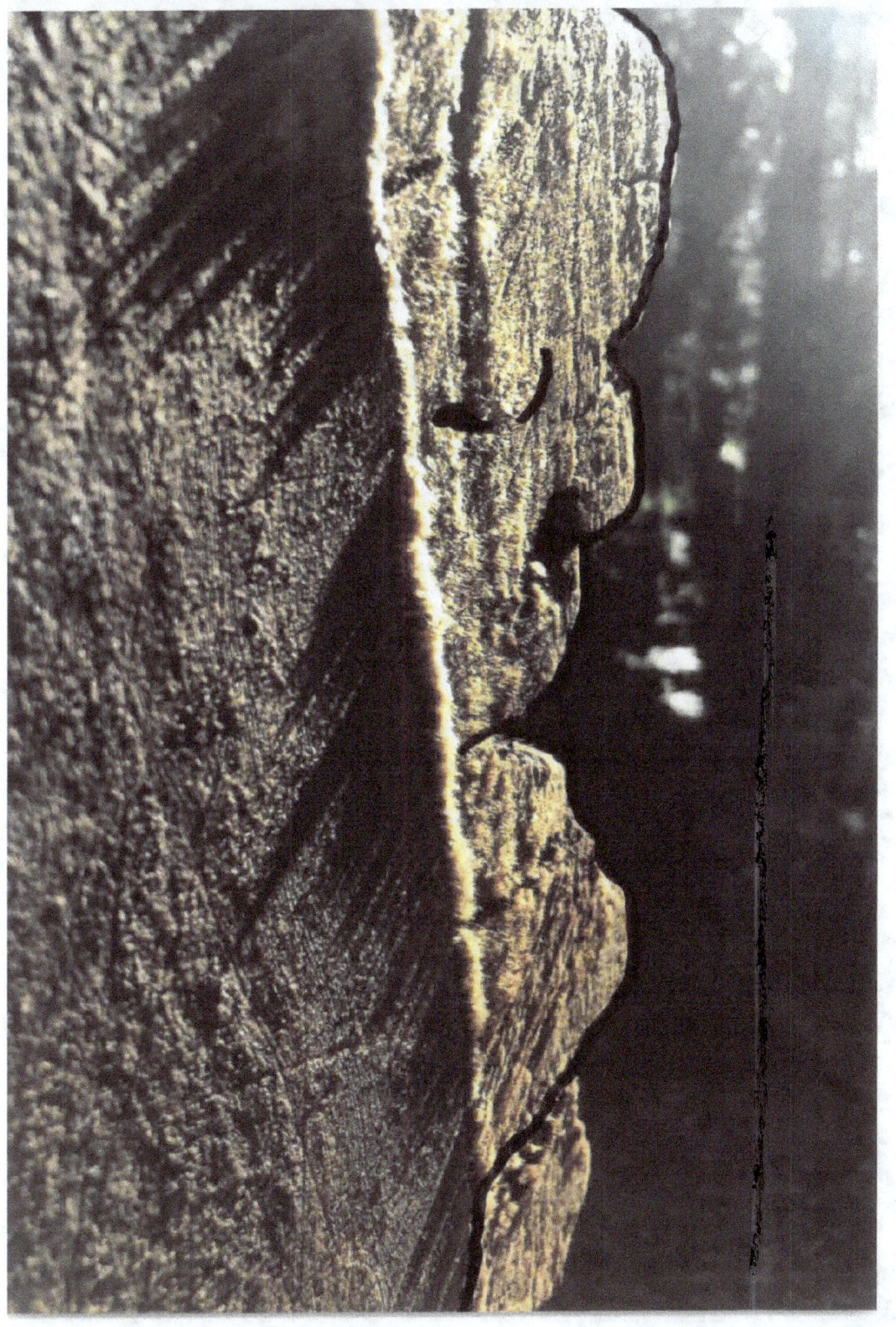

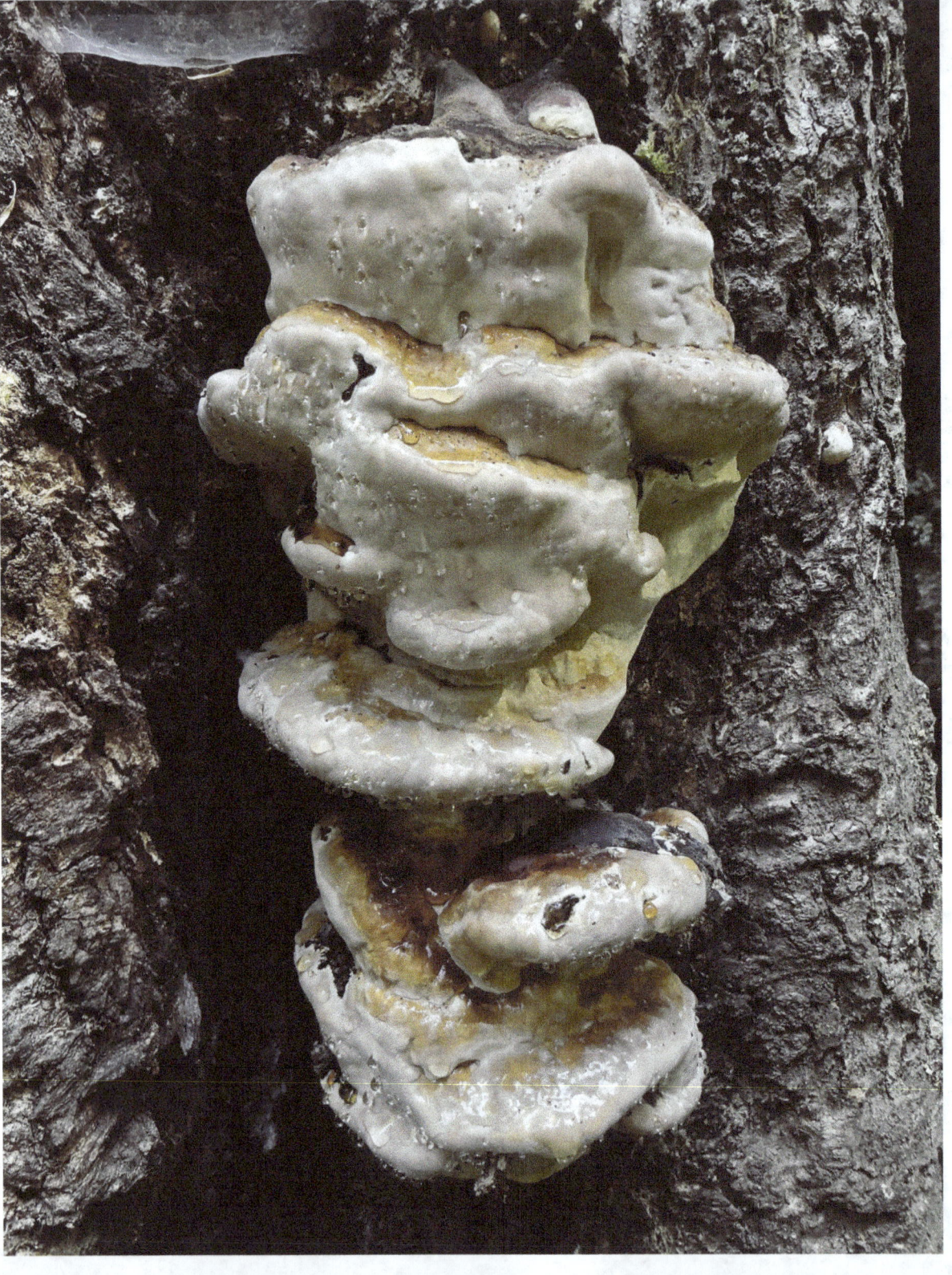

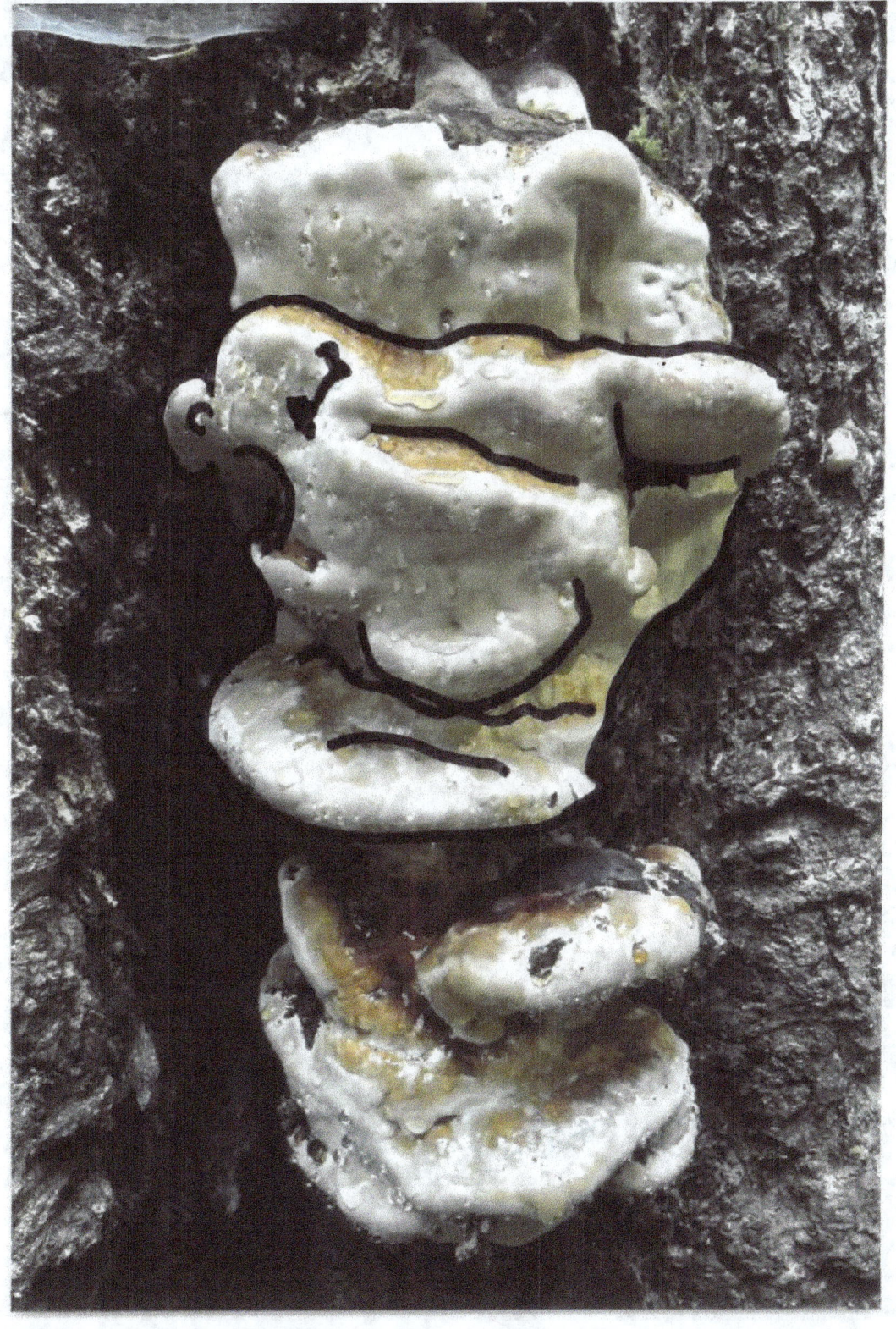

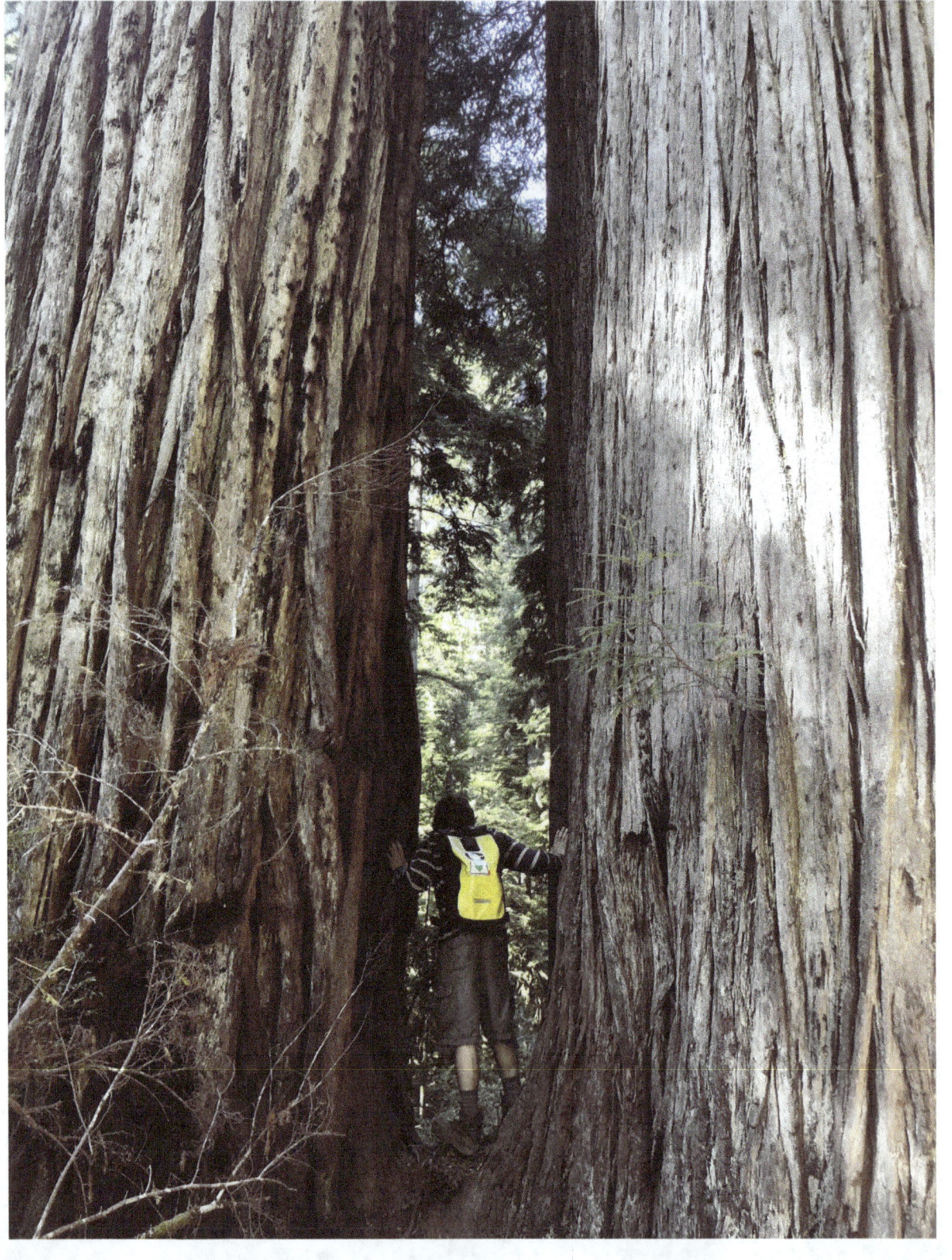

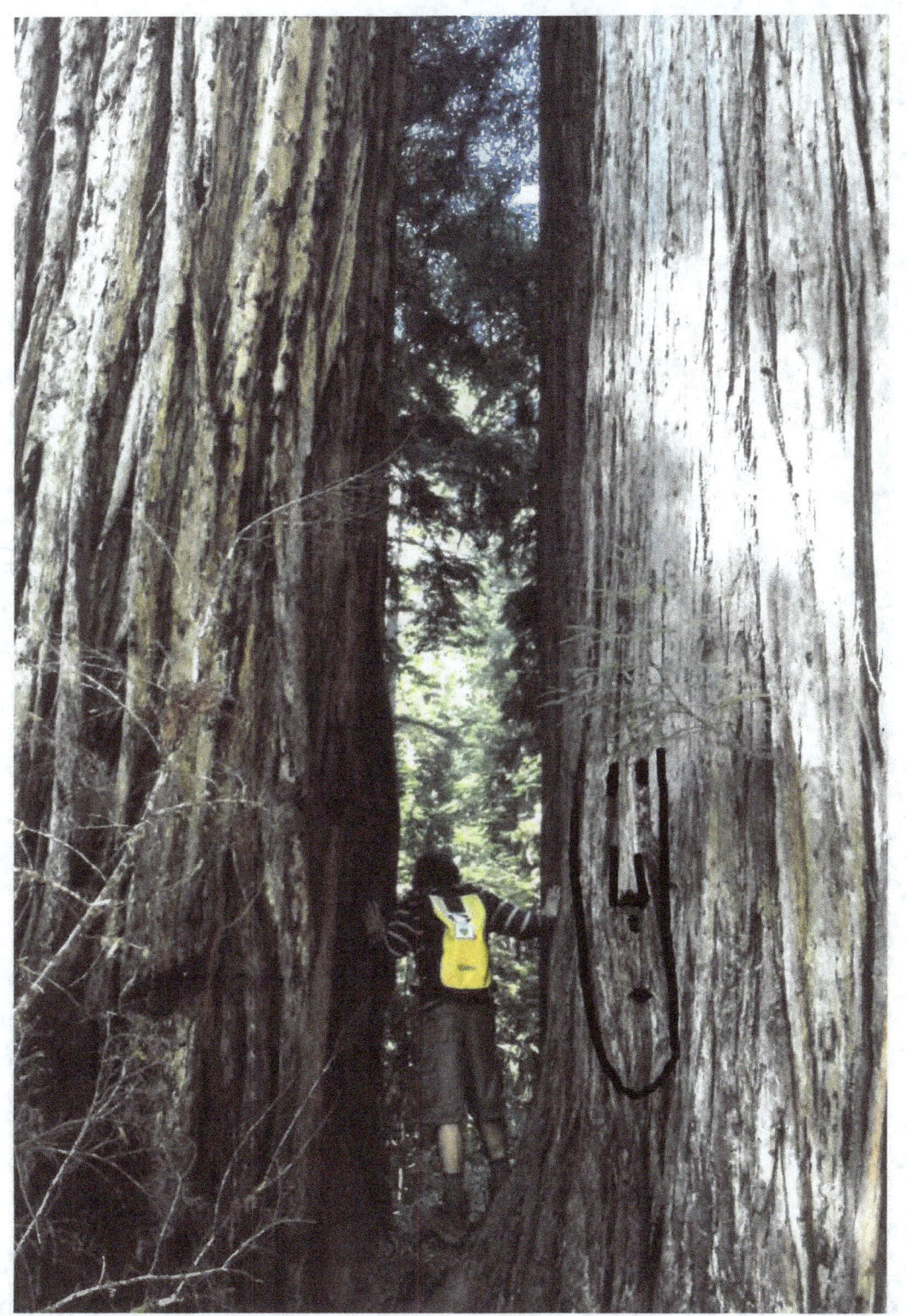

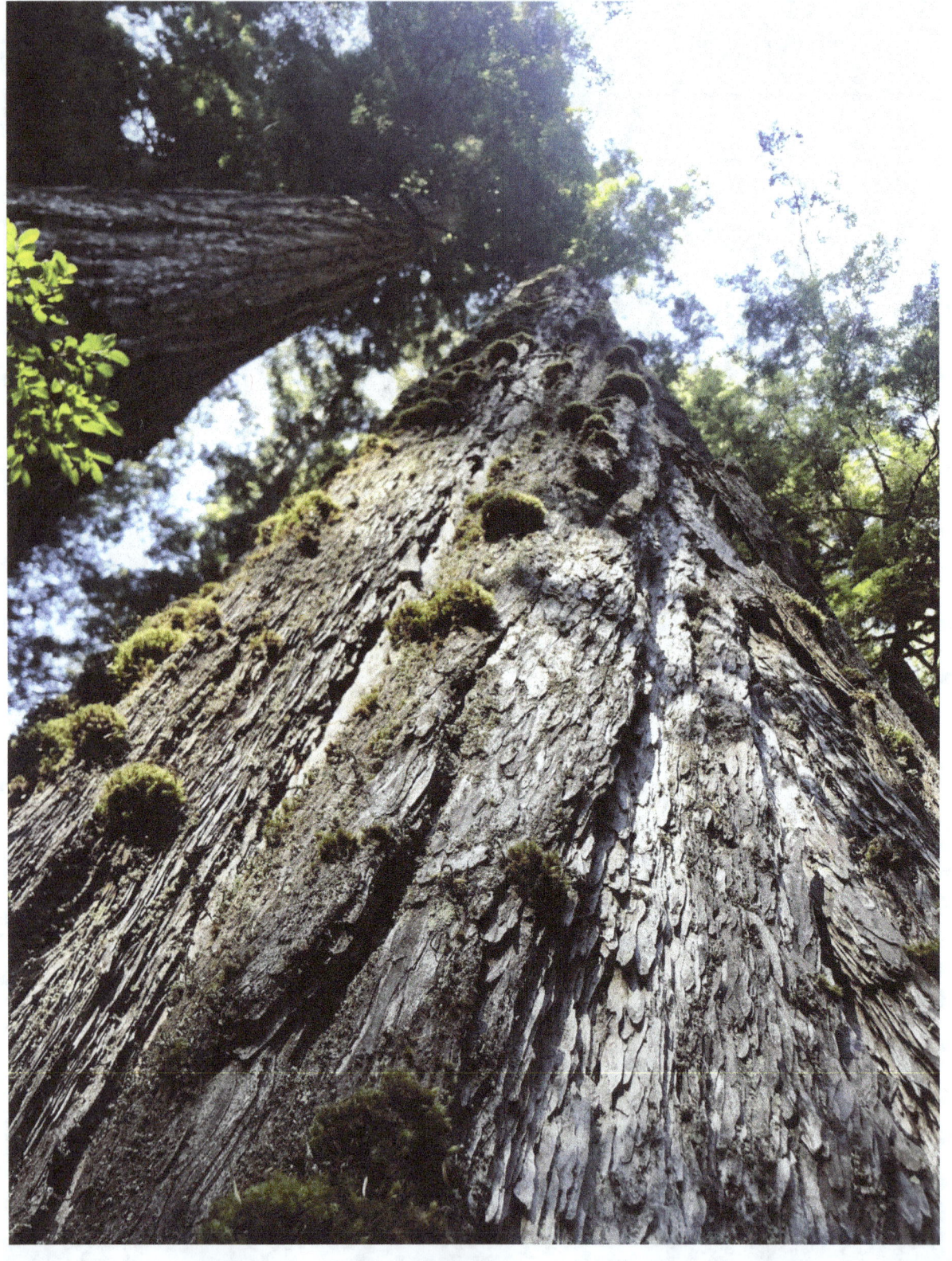

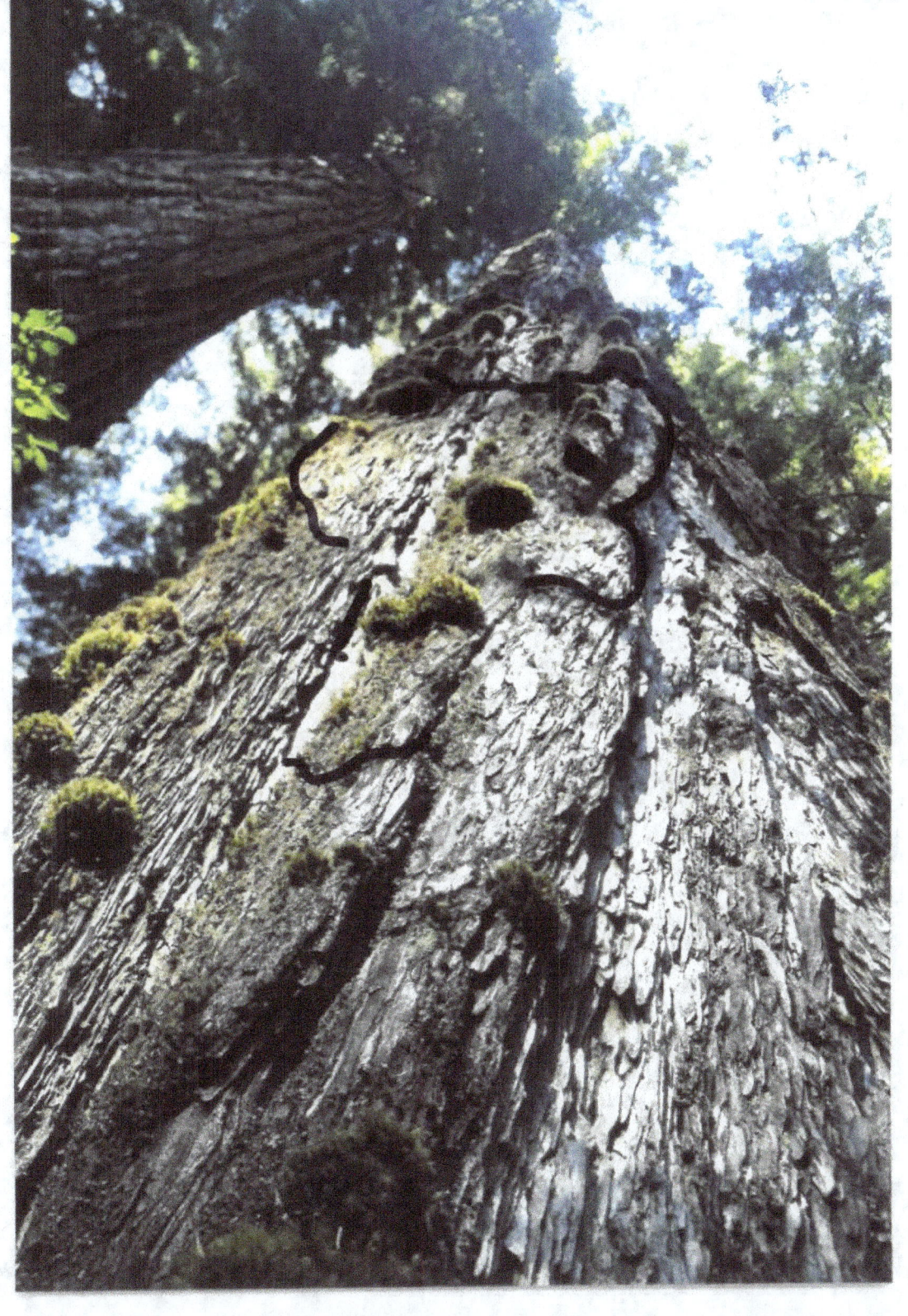

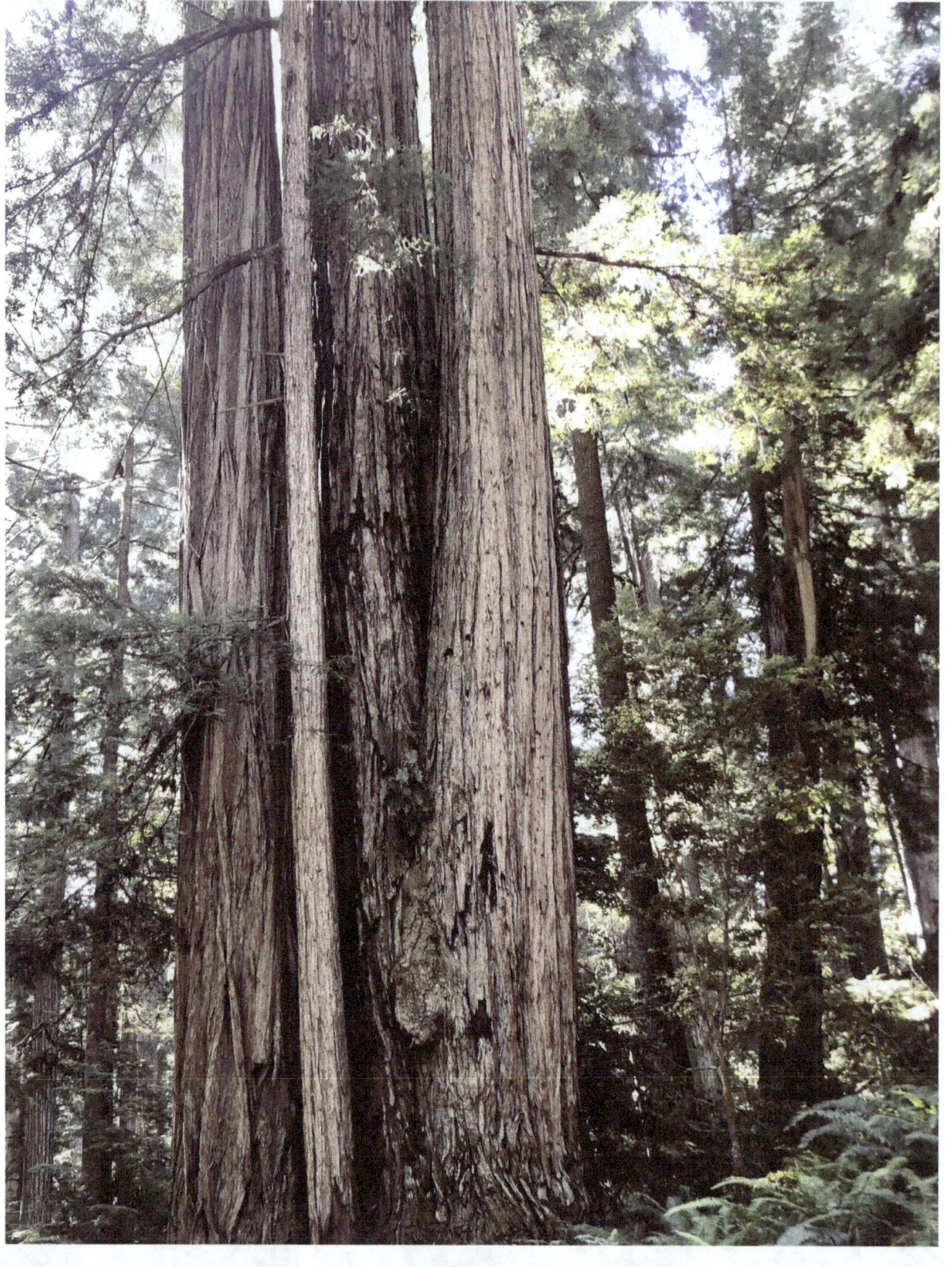

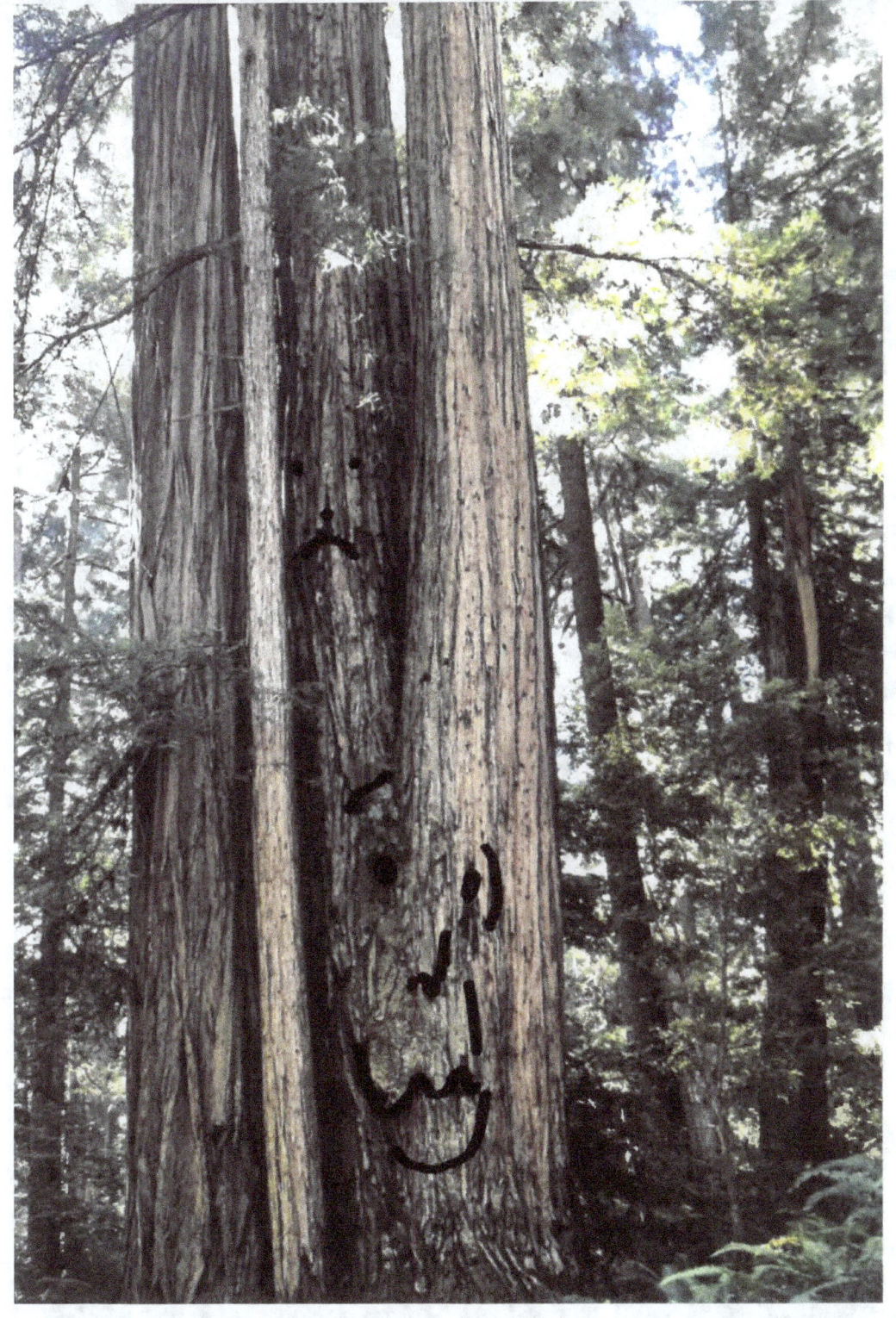

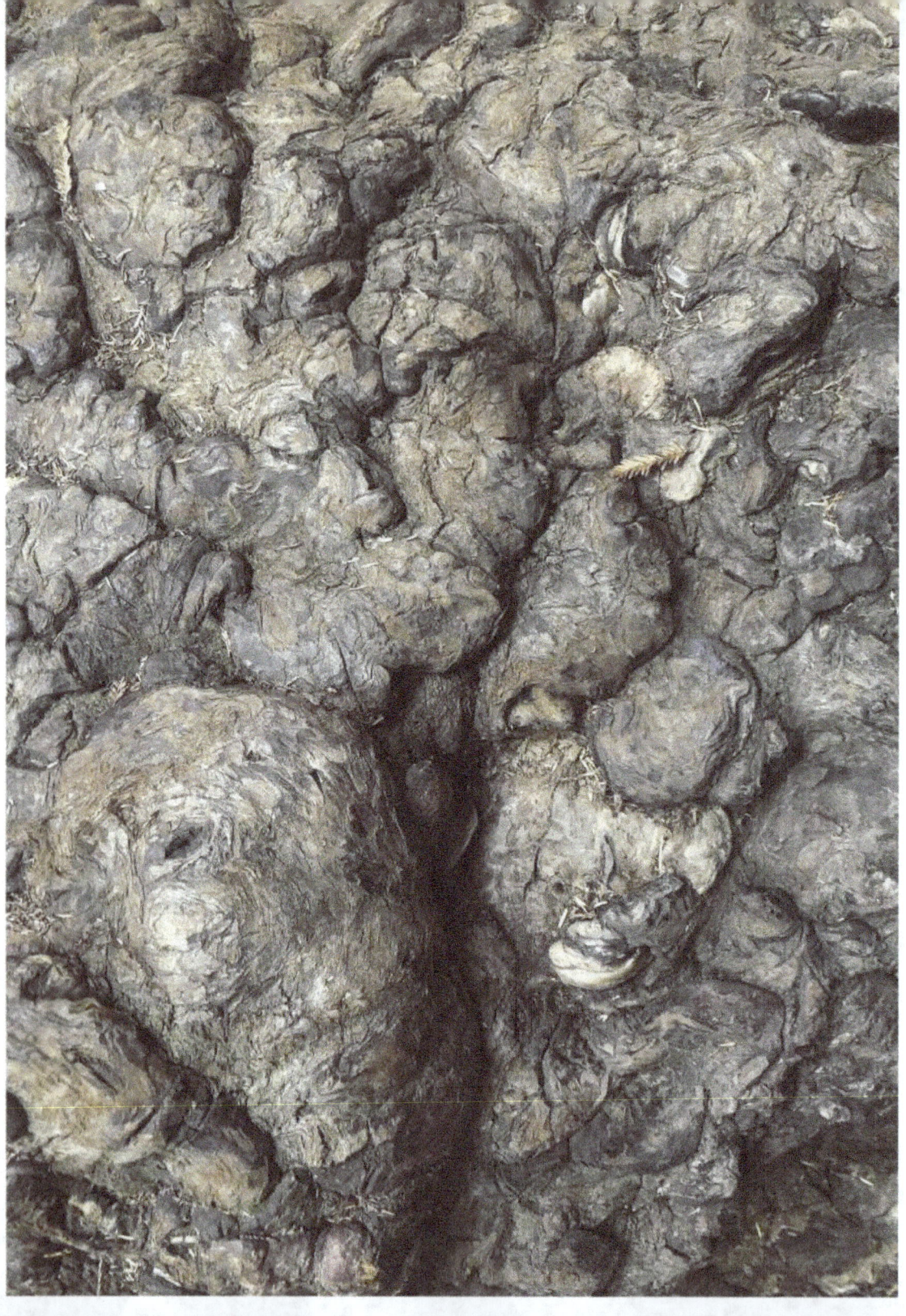

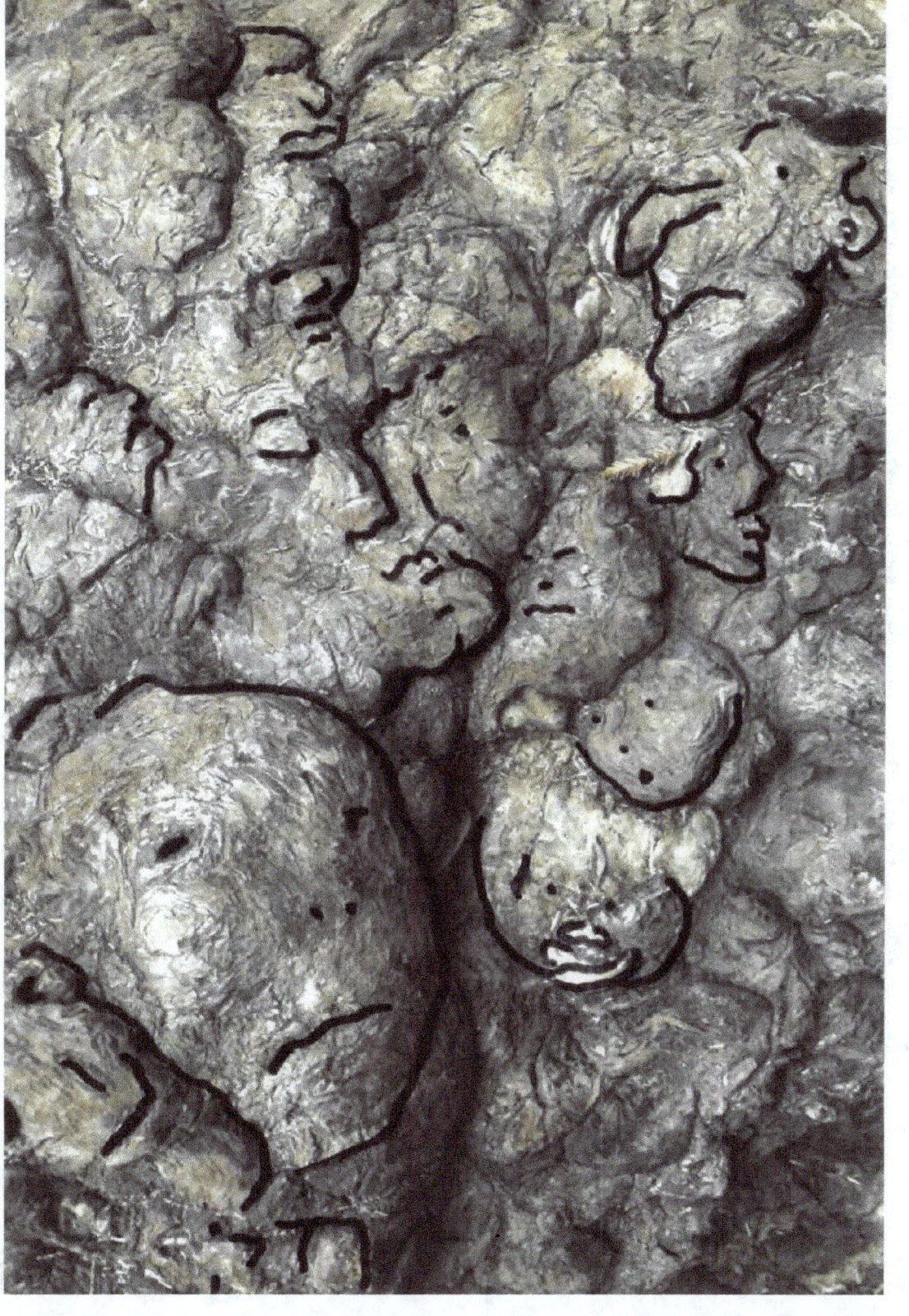

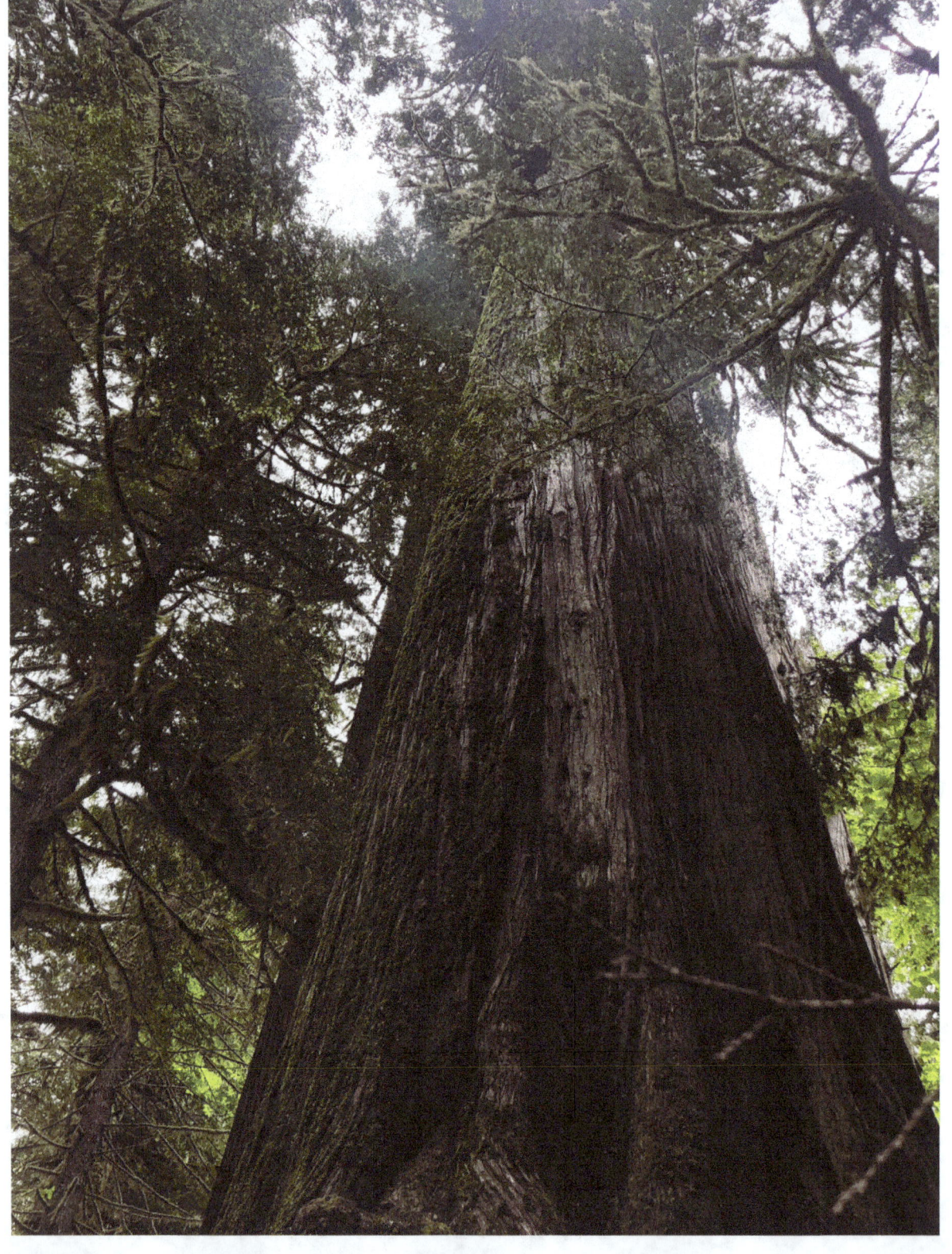

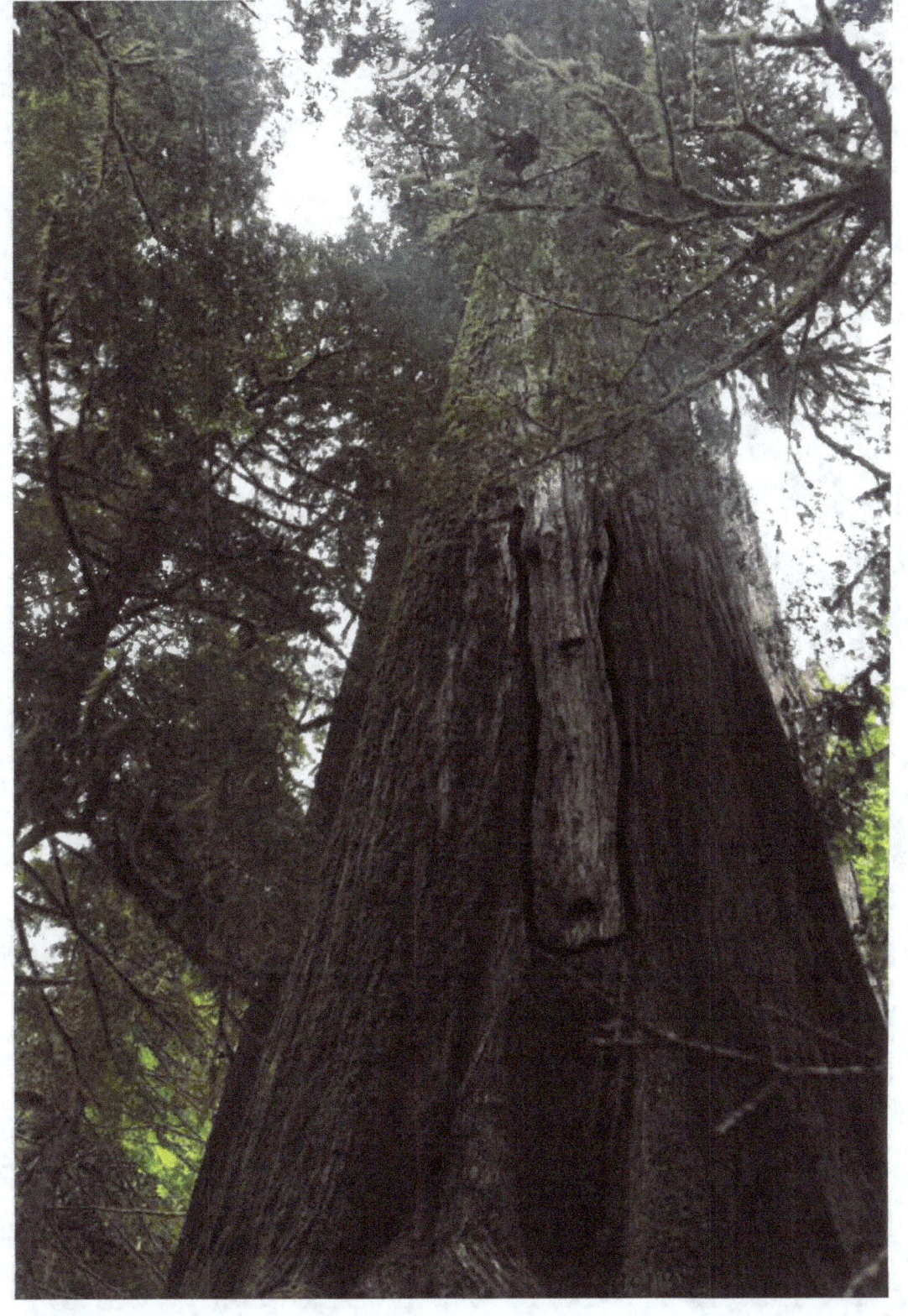

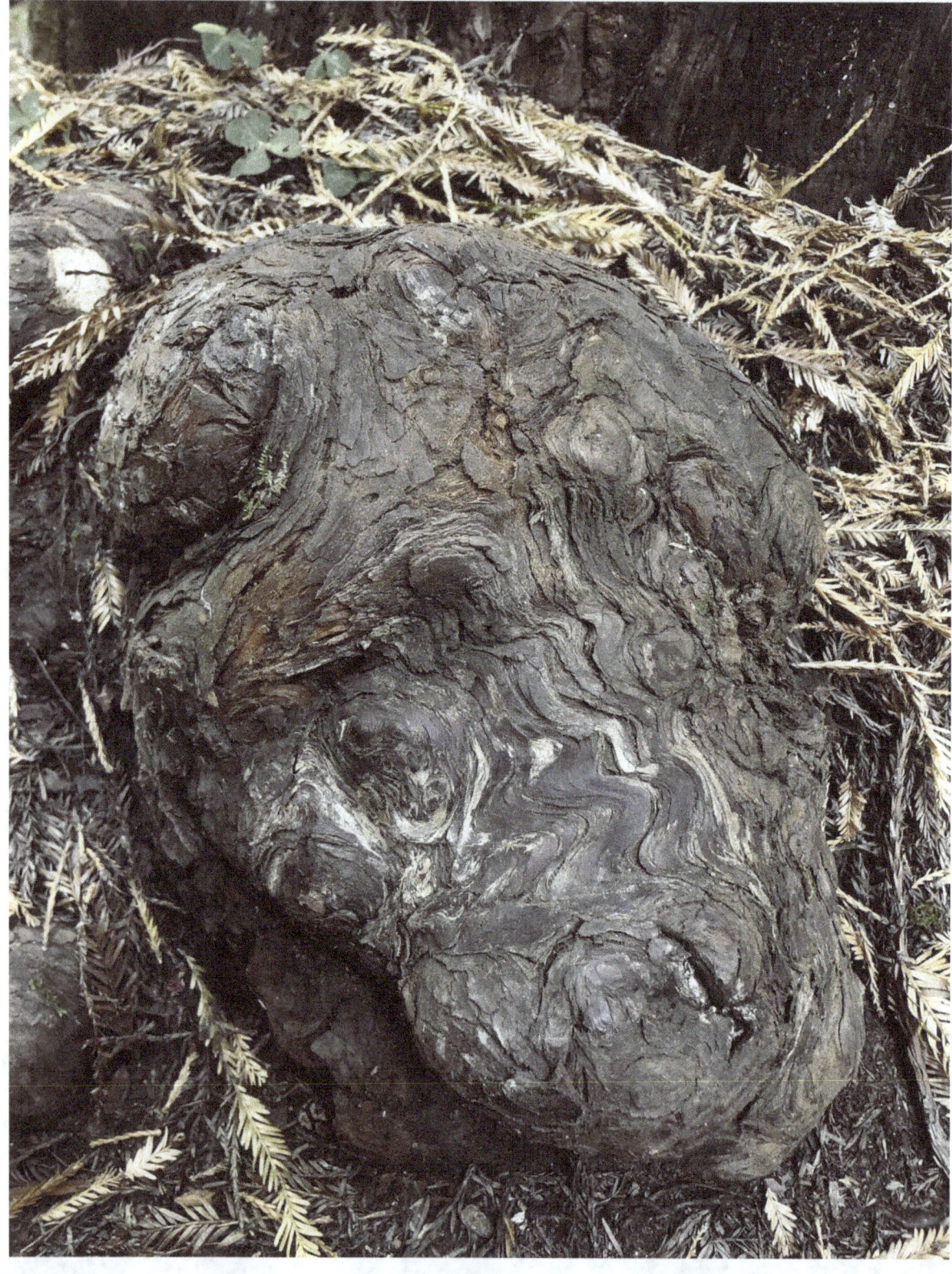

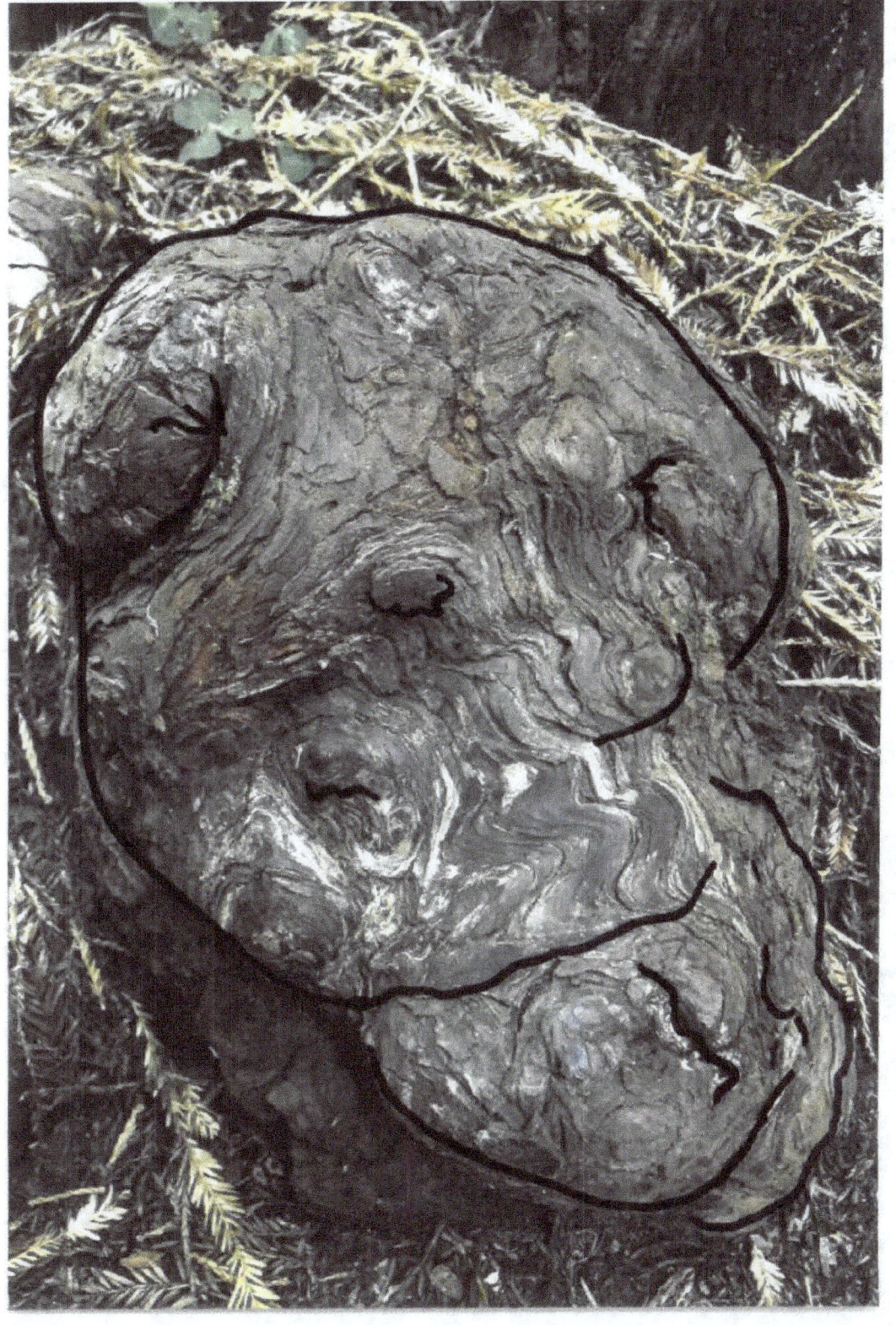

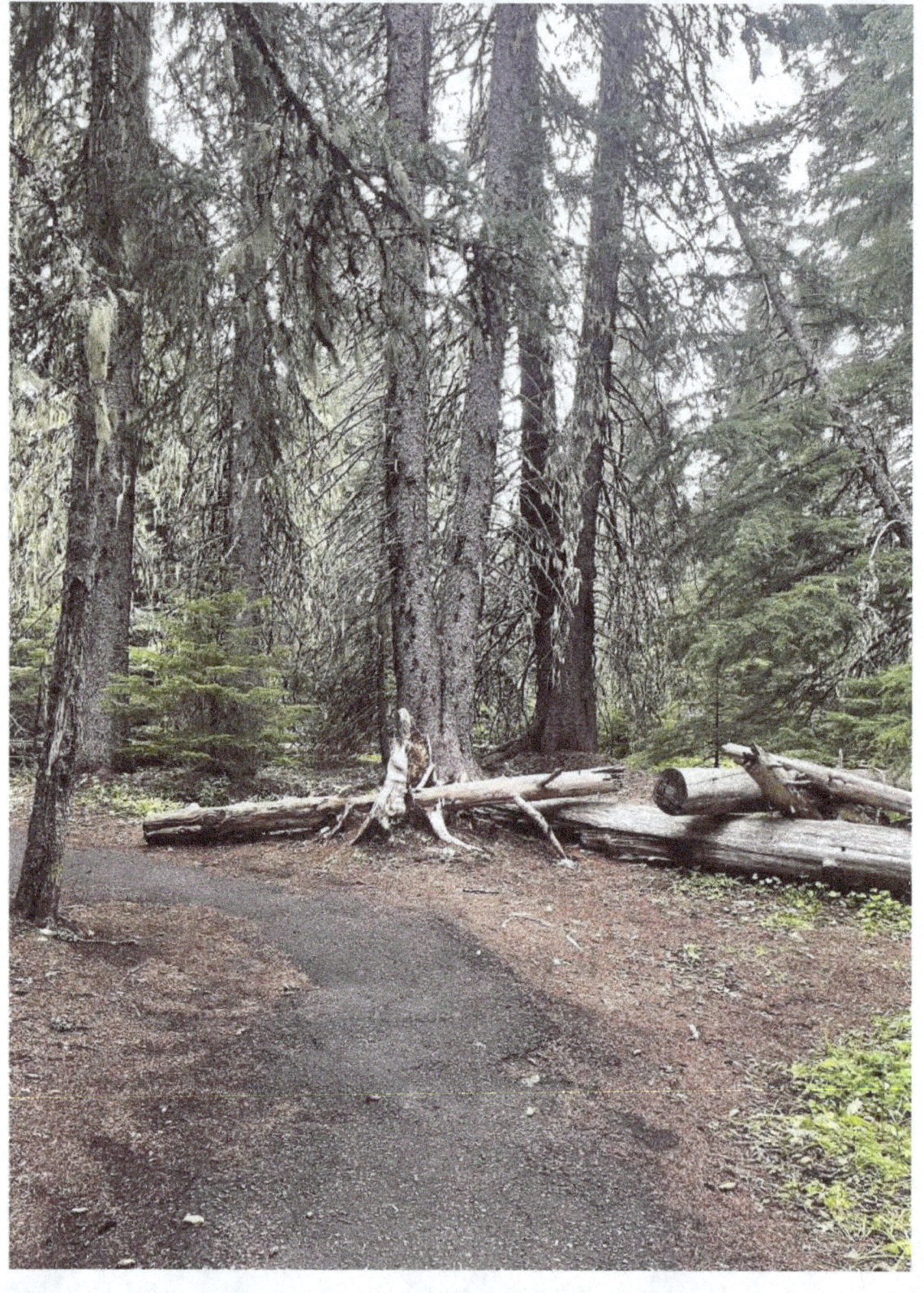

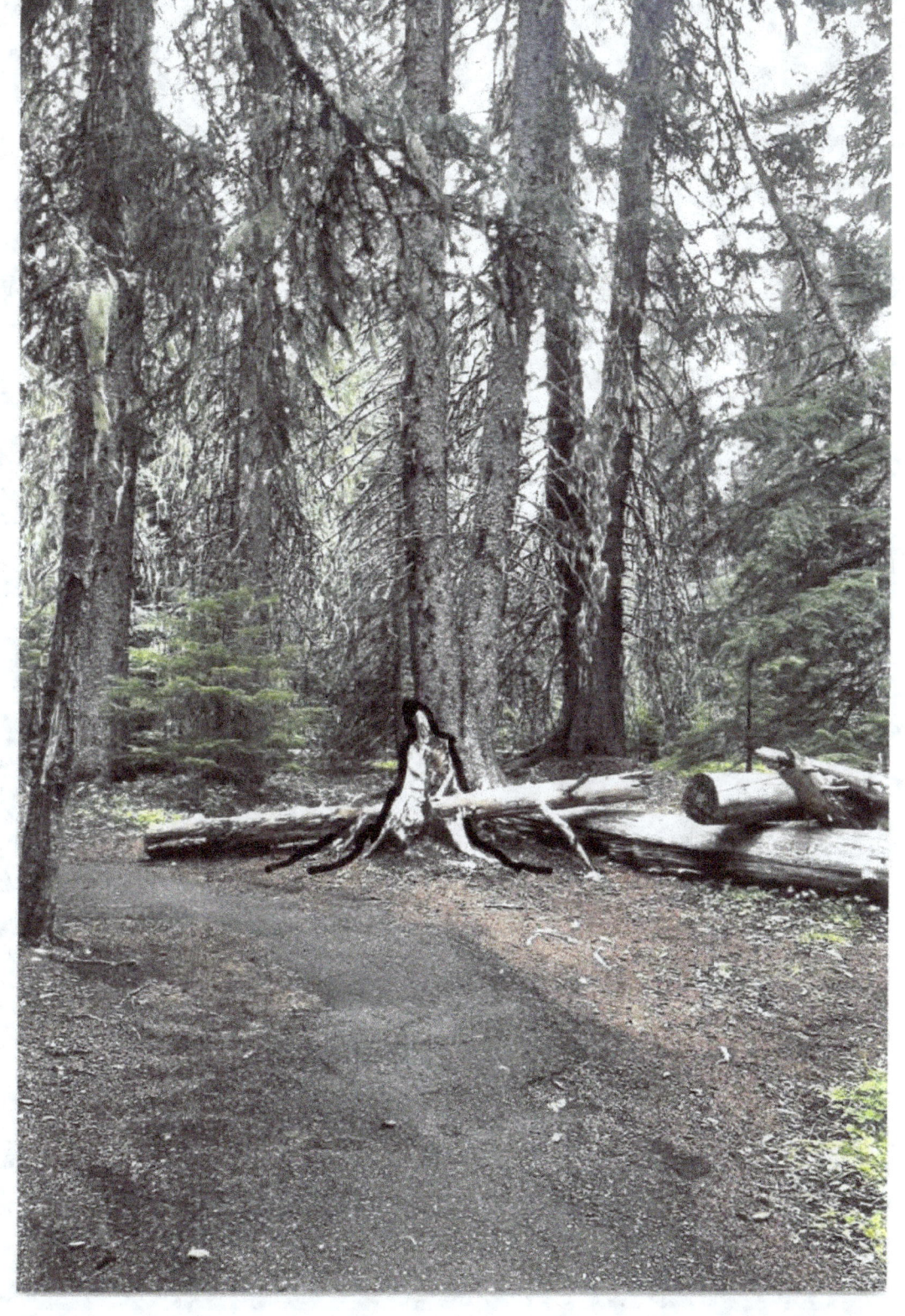

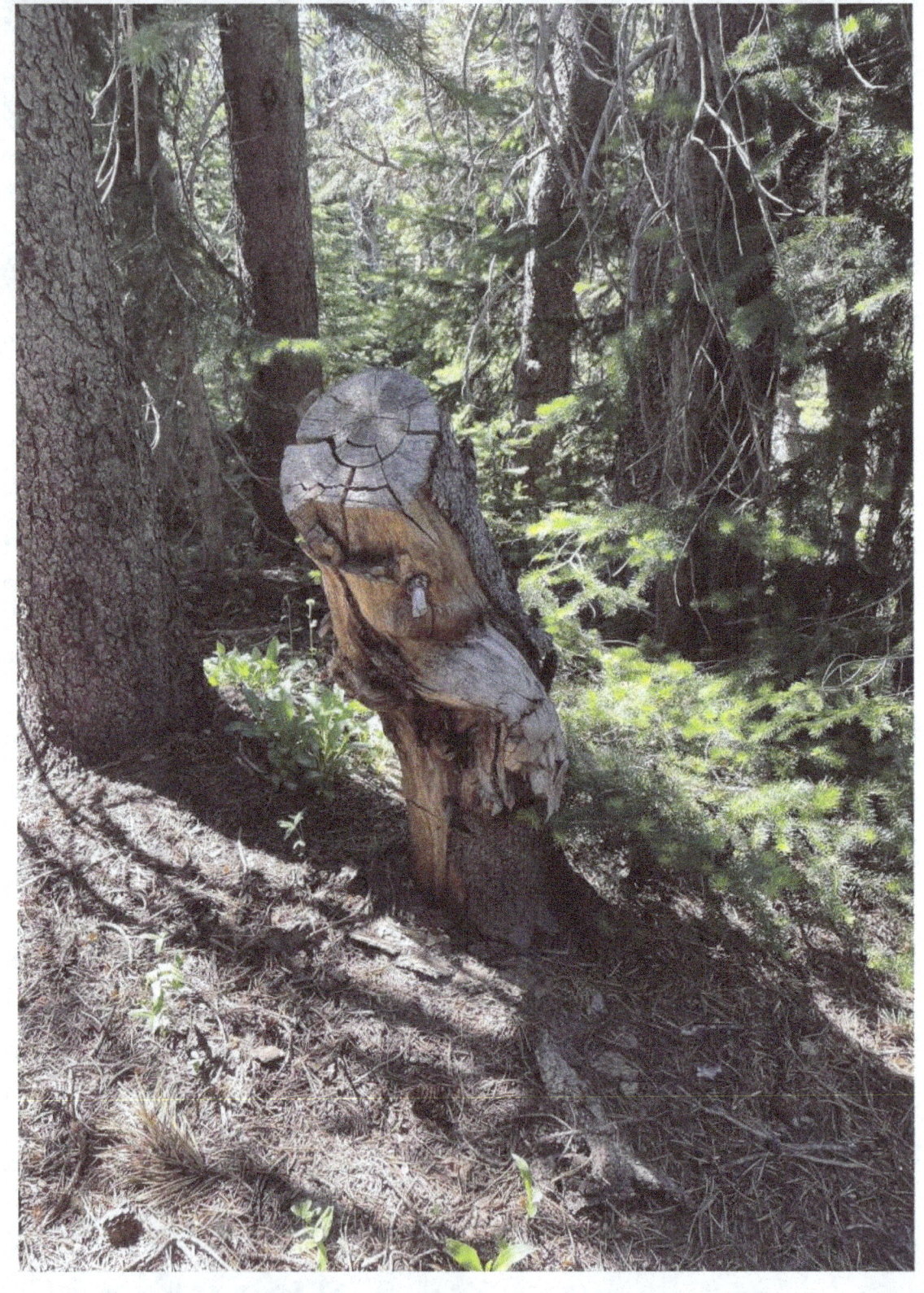

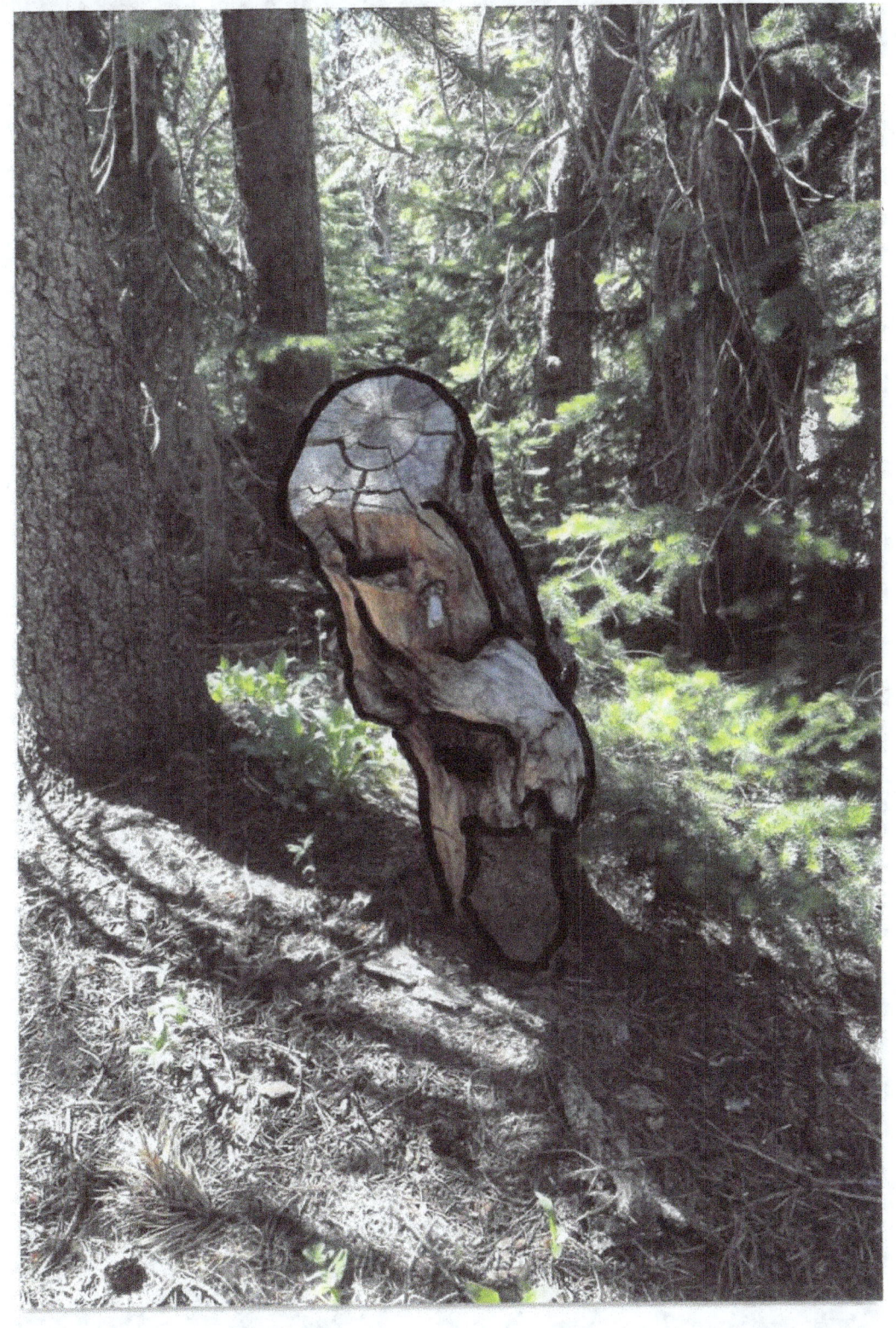

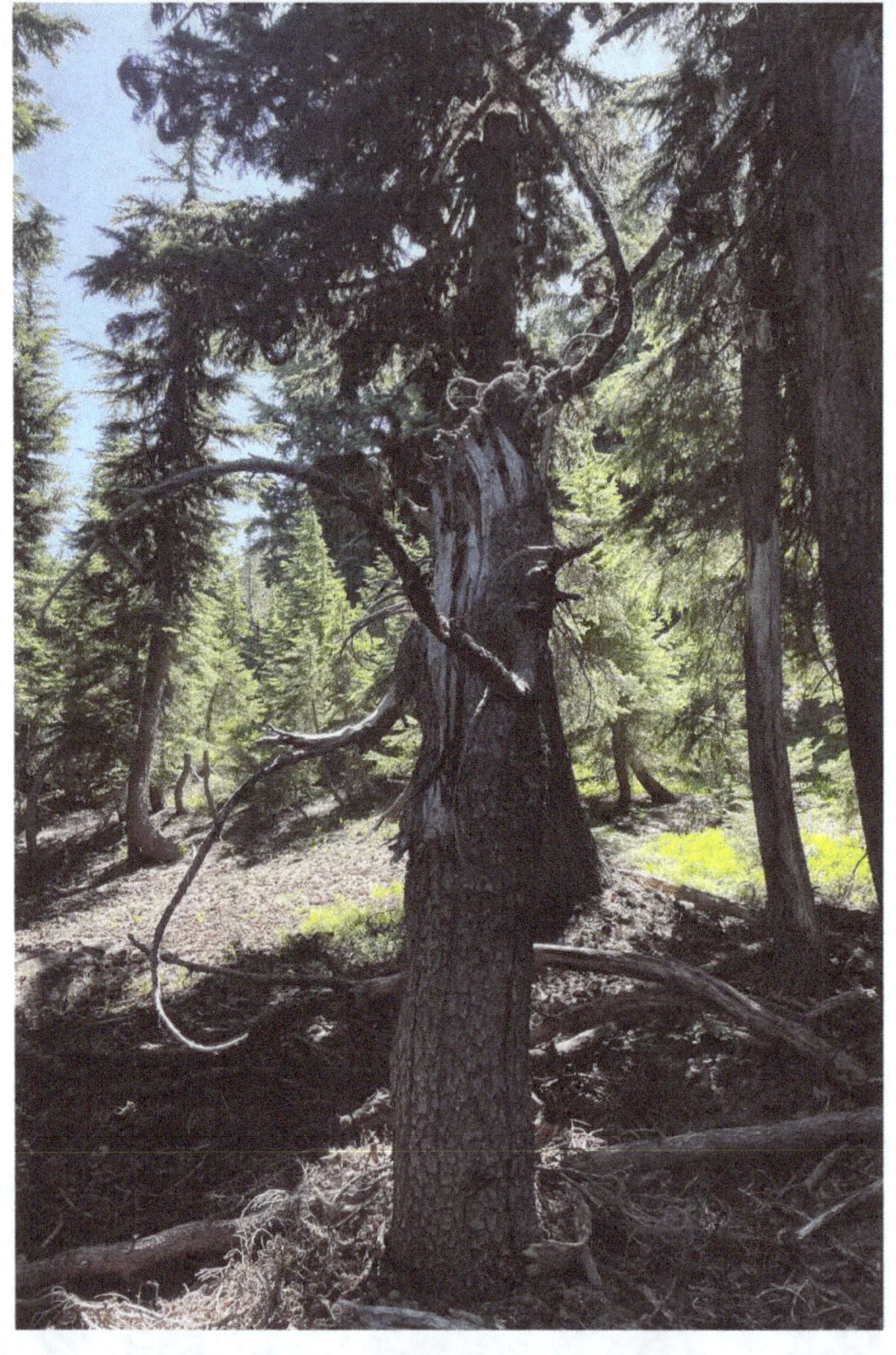

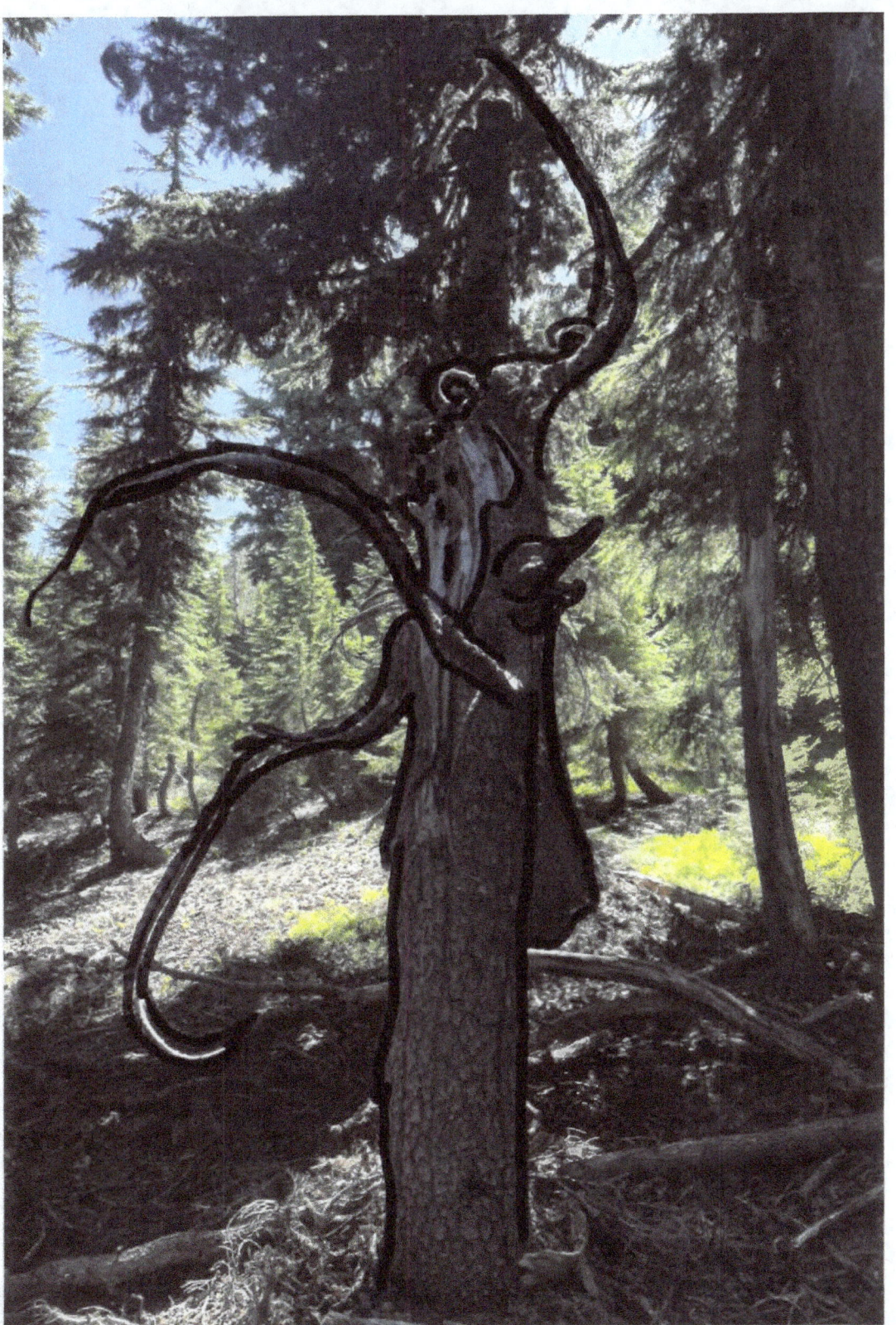